ATTIC BLACK-FIGURED POTTERY

ATTIC BLACK-FIGURED POTTERY

by

ROBERT S. FOLSOM

NOYES CLASSICAL STUDIES

NOYES PRESS
Park Ridge, New Jersey

Published in the United States by
NOYES PRESS
Noyes Building
Park Ridge, New Jersey 07656

Library of Congress Cataloging in Publication Data

Folsom, Robert Slade.
   Attic black-figured pottery.

   (Noyes classical studies)
   Bibliography: p.
   Includes index.
   1. Vase-painting, Greek. 2. Vases, Greek.
I. Title.
NK4648.F6   738.3'82'0938   75-13568
ISBN 0-8155-5035-9

PREFACE

In my *Handbook of Greek Pottery* I attempted to introduce Greek painted pottery of the period 1050 to 320 B.C. to the amateur interested in archaeology. I hoped to familiarize him with various shapes, from the well-known *amphora* to the less common *askos.* I hoped also to enable the reader to distinguish broadly among the products of Corinth, Laconia, East Greece, the Cyclades, and Attica and among the Protogeometric, Geometric, Archaic, Classical, and Hellenistic periods.

The present book develops one segment of the general subject of Greek pottery, the Athenian black-figure technique. In a companion volume, I plan to offer a similar survey of the Attic red-figure technique.

In presenting this book, I am well aware that nothing new is set forth. My purpose has been to summarize in one volume information collected from various scholarly works—most of which are out of print or expensive and usually accessible only in large libraries. My hope is to arouse in the reader an interest in Greek archaeology and, specifically, to make intelligible to him the rows of somber black-figured vases that he sees in museums throughout Europe and the United States.

Organizationally, this book may be regarded as composed of two parts. Chapters One and Two provide background while Chapters Three through Six trace the black-figure technique from its origins to its extinction. Appendices supplement the text, listing potters, love names, and painters of Panathenaic amphorae, and illustrating certain terms not previously explained in the text or glossary.

I have used notes sparsely, especially in Chapters Three through Six. Had I given credit every time it was possible, there would have been far too many references. For the sake of my readers, I may thus have slighted the authorities—if so, it is not because I do not acknowledge my debts to them. I hope they will accept my rather broad attributions with my sincere gratitude in lieu of more specific references.

Arlington, Va.   *Robert S.Folsom*
April, 1975

ACKNOWLEDGMENTS

Like my previous guide to ancient Greek pottery,* this book is a secondary work designed for the amateur and makes no pretense of providing original contributions in the field of archaeology. For its contents, I have relied on authorities in the field.

My greatest debt is to the late Sir John Davidson Beazley without whose works, notably his *Attic Black-figure Vase Painters, The Development of Attic Black-figure, Attic Black-figure: A Sketch* and *Paralipomena*, this book would have been impossible. In this connection, see the introductions to Appendices I to IV for more detailed acknowledgment of the extent of my indebtedness in connection with attribution of works to painters and potters and use of *kalos* and *kalé* names.

Miss C.H.E. Haspels' *Attic Black-figured Lekythoi* and Dietrich von Bothmer's article on Tyrrhenian vases in the *American Journal of Archaeology* were invaluable sources of information on these special types of black-figured work.

To Joseph Veach Noble I owe a very particular debt for his personal help with the section in my introduction dealing with colors as well as for the information contained in his book *The Techniques of Painted Attic Pottery*.

Shapes and Names of Athenian Vases, by the late Miss Gisela M.A. Richter and Miss Marjorie J. Milne, was of very special value in providing clear data and illustrations of the major shapes employed in Attic black-figured pottery.

Other important sources which I have used include Arias and Hirmer's *A History of Greek Vase Painting*, R.M. Cook's *Greek Painted Pottery* and Robertson's *Greek Painting*.

For certain aspects, particularly comments on the styles and distinctive characteristics of various painters, I have drawn on various other authorities as listed in the bibliography.

While citing my authorities and acknowledging my debt to each, l accept at the same time responsibility for errors of interpretation or fact.

Among individuals who have been of assistance I wish to thank Miss Yvonne Diaz, Mrs. A. Allen King, Mrs. Helen Eidsness and Mrs. Fernande Fanfant, all of whom have struggled with my manuscript. Lucy E. Weier's assistance was invaluable in obtaining certain key photographs.

To the following I am indebted for their courtesy and time in permitting me behind the scenes in various museums or for giving me advice: Dr. Eugene Vanderpool (of the American School of Classical Studies and the Agora Museum of Athens), Dr. Photis Petsas (then Ephor of Antiquities in Thessaloniki), Dr. Vassos Karageorghis (Director of the Cyprus Archaeological Service), Professor David Mitten (of the Fogg Museum at Harvard University), Miss Anna Booth (of the Rhode Island School of Design, Providence), Dr. Cornelius Vermeule and Dr. Emily Vermeule (of the Boston Museum of Fine Arts), Miss Barbara Rumpf (of the Seattle Art Museum), Dr. Henry P. Maynard (of the Wadsworth Atheneum in Hartford) and Mr. E. R. Gallagher (Registrar of the Palace of the Legion of Honor in San Francisco).

To Professor William Sanford (of the University of Ife, Nigeria) and to Horace D. Ashton (of Port-au-Prince) I wish to express appreciation for numerous helpful suggestions.

Above all I owe a debt to my wife, Florence, for reading and rereading my manuscript and for invaluable advice.

*Folsom, Robert S., *Handbook of Greek Pottery: A Guide for Amateurs*. Faber and Faber Ltd., London, 1967.

CONTENTS

LIST OF PLATES AND FIGURES

Plates

In choosing photographs, I have sought to illustrate the developments and trends of the black-figure technique by means of seldom-published vases whenever feasible. I have also relied heavily on vases located in American museums. In some cases, however—the François Vase and the Exekias Vatican amphora are examples—exclusion of famous works in European museums would have meant substitution of an inferior item or failure to provide the reader with an appropriate example. In brief, I have sought to combine the best with what I hope will be new to the reader.

3a. Bf dinos fragment: Ht. of zone with horses 8 cm., by Sophilos, ca. 580–570 B.C., Athens 15499.
Photo: National Archaeological Museum, Athens.

3b. Bf Komast cup: Ht. 9.5 cm., diam. of bowl 20.9 cm., by the KX Painter, ca. 590–570 B.C., New York 22.139.22 (Rogers Fund, 1922).
Photo: The Metropolitan Museum of Art, New York.

3c. Bf skyphos: Ht. 10 cm., by the KX Painter, ca. 590–570 B.C., Athens 528.
Photo: National Archaeological Museum, Athens.

3d. Bf Siana cup: Ht. 13 cm., diam. of bowl 24.5 cm., by the C Painter, mid-sixth century B.C., New York 01.8.6 (GR 521) (Purchase 1901).
Photo: The Metropolitan Museum of Art, New York.

4a. Bf neck-amphora: Tyrrhenian type, Ht. 38.7 cm., by the Timiades Painter, ca. 575–550 B.C., New York L 66.5 (Collection of Dean K. Boorman).
Photo: The Metropolitan Museum of Art, New York.

4b. Bf amphora: Ht. 38.3 cm., unattributed, ca. 560–550 B.C. New York 26.60.45 (Fletcher Fund, 1926).
Photo: The Metropolitan Museum of Art, New York.

4c. Bf oval lekythos: Ht. 17.5 cm., by the Pharos Painter, ca. 575–550 B.C., New York 75.2.10 (GR 541) (Gift of Samuel G. Ward, 1875).
Photo: The Metropolitan Museum of Art, New York.

4d. Bf shoulder lekythos: Ht. 18.7 cm., unattributed, mid-sixth century B.C., New York 30.115.27 (The Theodore M. Davis Collection, Bequest of Theodore M. Davis 1915).
Photo: The Metropolitan Museum of Art, New York.

5a. Bf volute-krater: Ht. 66 cm., "The François Vase", by Kleitias, ca. 570 B.C., Florence 4209.
Photo: Soprintendenza Antichita, Florence.

5b. Bf dinos: Ht. 49 cm., by the Painter of Acropolis 606, ca. 575–550 B.C., Athens 15116.
Photo: National Archaeological Museum, Athens.

5c. Bf kantharos fragment: Ht. 15 cm., by Nearchos, ca. 575–550 B.C., Athens Acr. 611.
Photo: National Archaeological Museum, Athens.

5d. Bf column-krater: Ht. 55.9 cm., by Lydos, ca. 550–540 B.C., New York 31.11.11 (Fletcher, Fund 1931).
Photo: The Metropolitan Museum of Art, New York.

6a. Bf amphora: Ht. 39 cm., by the Amasis Painter, ca. 550–540 B.C., New York 06.1021.69 (Rogers Fund, 1906).
Photo: The Metropolitan Museum of Art, New York.

6b. Bf amphora: Ht. 41.4 cm., by the Affecter, ca. 550–530 B.C., New York 18.145.15 (Rogers fund, 1918).
Photo: The Metropolitan Museum of Art, New York.

6c. Bf neck-hydria: Ht. 32.5 cm., by the painter known as "Elbows Out", mid-sixth century B.C., Boston 95-62 (Perkins Collection).
Photo: The Museum of Fine Arts, Boston.

6d. Bf amphora: Ht. 40.1 cm., by the Swing Painter (his namepiece), mid-sixth century B.C., Boston 98.918 (H.L. Pierce Fund).
Photo: The Museum of Fine Arts, Boston.

7a. Bf amphora: Ht. as restored 37.8 cm., attributed to Group E, ca. 540 B.C., New York 56.171.11 (Fletcher Fund, 1956).
Photo: The Metropolitan Museum of Art, New York.

7b. Bf neck-amphora: Ht. 47 cm., by Exekias, ca. 540 B.C., New York (17.230.14ab—(Rogers Fund, 1917).
Photo: The Metropolitan Museum of Art, New York.

7c. Bf. amphora: Ht. 61 cm., by Exekias, ca. 540–530 B.C., Vatican 344.
Photo: Archivio Fotografico, Gall. Mus. Vatican.

7d. Bf neck-amphora: Ht. 41.3 cm., by Exekias, ca. 530 B.C. London B 210.
Photo: The British Museum, London.

8a. Bf lip-cup: Ht. 19.6 cm., diam. of bowl 28.5 cm., by the Phrynos Painter, ca. 550 B.C., London B 424
Photo: The British Museum, London.

8b. Bf. lip-cup: Ht. 17.5 cm., diam. of bowl 21.7 cm., by the Tleson Painter and the potter Tleson, ca. 550–525 B.C., New York 55.11.13 (Purchase, 1955, Christos G. Bastis Gift).
Photo: The Metropolitan Museum of Art.

8c. Bf. band-cup: Ht. 16.4 cm. diam. of bowl 28.4 cm., unattributed, ca. 550–520 B.C., New York 17.230.5 (Rogers Fund 1917).
Photo: The Metropolitan Museum of Art, New York.

8d. Bf. Cassel cup: Ht. 8.7 cm. diam. of bowl 13.4 cm., unattributed, ca. 550–525 B.C., New York 248.16.
Photo: The Metropolitan Museum of Art, New York.

9a. Bf. Droop cup: Ht. 128 cm., Diam. of bowl 25.4 cm., attributed to the Group of Rhodes 12264, ca. 550–525 B.C., New York 06.1021.161 (Rogers Fund, 1906).
Photo: The Metropolitan Museum of Art, New York.

9b. Bf proto-A cup: Ht. 11.4 cm. diam. of bowl 20.3 cm., by the Painter of Louvre F28, mid-sixth century B.C., New York 06.1097 (Rogers Fund, 1906).
Photo: The Metropolitan Museum of Art, New York.

9c. Bf. Type A or eye-cup: Ht. 11.9 cm. diam. of bowl 30.5 cm. unattributed, ca. 525 B.C., Rhode Island School of Design 63.048.
Photo: Museum of Art, Rhode Island School of Design, Providence.

9d. Bf one-piece (Type B) cup: Ht. 6.5 cm. diam. of bowl 14.9 cm., in the manner of the Haimon Painter, ca. 500–475 B.C., New York 41.162.232 (Rogers Fund, 1941).
Photo: The Metropolitan Museum of Art, New York.

10a. Bf. stemless kylix: Ht. 7 cm. Diam. of bowl 18.2 cm., unattributed, late third of 6th century B.C., de Young 713.
Photo: The M.H. de Young Memorial Museum, San Francisco.

10b. Bf neck-amphora, Nikosthenic type: Ht. 28.6 cm., unattributed, but signed by the potter Nikosthenes, late 6th century B.C., Rhode Island School of Design 23.303.
Photo: Museum of Art, Rhode Island School of Design, Providence.

10c. Bf. amphora: Ht. 53.2 cm., by the Lysippides Painter, ca. 530–520 B.C., New York 58.32 (Gift of Colonel and Mrs. Lewis Landes, 1958).
Photo: The Metropolitan Museum of Art, New York.

10d. Bf neck-hydria: Ht. 51.1 cm., by the Antimenes Painter, ca. 520–500 B.C., Minneapolis 61.59 (The John R. Van Derlip Fund).
Photo: The Minneapolis Institute of Art, Minneapolis.

11a. Bf neck-hydria: Ht. 54.1 cm., attributed to The Leagros Group, ca. 515–510 B.C., New York 56.171.29 (Fletcher Fund, 1956).
Photo: The Metropolitan Museum of Art, New York.

11b. Bf amphora: Ht. 51.1 cm., by the Rycroft Painter, ca. 525 B.C., New York 06.1021.67 (Rogers Fund, 1906).
Photo: The Metropolitan Museum of Art, New York.

11c. Bf amphora: Ht. 39.2 cm., by the BMN Painter, ca. 540 B.C., Boston 60.1 (Otis Norcross Fund).
Photo: The Museum of Fine Arts, Boston.

11d. Bf. neck-hydria: Ht. (with handle) 47 cm., by Psiax, ca. 530–500 B.C., Hartford 1961.8 (Ella Gallup Sumner and Mary Catlin Sumner Collection).
Photo: The Wadsworth Atheneum, Hartford (by E. Irving Blomstrann).

12a. Bf loutrophoros: Ht. 43.5 cm., unattributed, late sixth century B.C., Cleveland 27.145 (Purchase, Charles W. Harkness Fund).
Photo: The Cleveland Museum of Art, Cleveland.

12b. Bf oinochoe: Ht. 23 cm., unattributed, ca. 500–450 B.C., Fogg 1927.154.
Photo: The Fogg Art Museum, Harvard University, Cambridge.

12c. Bf lekythos: Ht. 27.7 cm., by the Gela Painter, ca. 500 B.C., Boston 93.100 (Gift of E.P. Warren).
Photo: The Museum of Fine Arts, Boston.

12d. Bf neck-amphora: Ht. 26.7 cm., by the Edinburgh Painter, early fifth century B.C., New York 56.49.1 (Gift of El Conde de Lagunillos, 1956).
Photo: The Metropolitan Museum of Art, New York.

13a. Bf lekythos: Ht. 14.8 cm., by the Marathon Painter, ca. 490 B.C., New York 75.2.21 (Gift of Samuel G. Ward, 1875).
Photo: The Metropolitan Museum of Art, New York.

13b. Bf lekythos: Ht. 17.9 cm., by the Sappho Painter, ca. 500–490 B.C., New York 41.162.29 (Rogers Fund, 1941).
Photo: The Metropolitan Museum of Art, New York.

13c. Bf lekythos: Ht. 25.4 cm., by the Diosphos Painter, ca. 485–460 B.C., New York 06.1070 (Rogers Fund, 1906).
Photo: The Metropolitan Museum of Art, New York.

13d. Bf. skyphos: Ht. 16.2 cm., diam. of bowl 22.4 cm., by the Theseus Painter, ca. 500 B.C., New York 17.230.9 (Rogers Fund, 1917).
Photo: The Metropolitan Museum of Art, New York.

14a. Bf. lekythos: Ht. 34.6 cm., by the Athena Painter, ca. 480 B.C., New York 07.286.68 (Rogers Fund, 1907).
Photo: The Metropolitan Museum of Art, New York.

14b. Bf lekythos: Ht. 34.6 cm., by the Haimon Painter, early fifth century B.C., New York 41.162.13 (Rogers Fund, 1941).
Photo: The Metropolitan Museum of Art, New York.

14c. Bf "chimney" lekythos: Ht. 27.8 cm., by the Emporion Painter, ca. 470 B.C., New York 41.162.119 (Rogers Fund, 1941)
Photo: The Metropolitan Museum of Art, New York.

14d. Bf Panathenaic amphora: Ht. 61 cm., "The Burgon Vase", attributed to the Burgon Group, ca. 570–560 B.C., London B 130
Photo: The British Museum, London.

15a. Bf Panathenaic amphora: Ht. 62.2 cm., by the Euphiletos Painter, ca. 520 B.C., New York 14.130.12 (Rogers Fund, 1914).
Photo: The Metropolitan Museum of Art, New York.

15b. Bf Panathenaic amphora: Ht. 64.8 cm., attributed to the Leagros Group, ca. 510 B.C., New York 07.286.80 (Rogers Fund, 1907).
Photo: The Metropolitan Museum of Art, New York.

15c. Bf Panathenaic amphora: Ht. 64.8 cm., by the Kleophrades Painter, ca. 500 B.C., New York 07.286.79 (Rogers Fund, 1907)
Photo: The Metropolitan Museum of Art, New York.

15d. Bf Panathenaic amphora: Ht. 73.9 cm., attributed to the Kuban Group, end of the fifth century B.C., London B 605.
Photo: The British Museum, London.

16a. Bf Panathenaic amphora: Ht. 71.2 cm., attributed to the Polyzelos Group, ca. 366 B.C., London B 604.
Photo: The British Museum.

16b. Bf Panathenaic amphora: Ht. 81.3 cm., unattributed, ca. 340–339 B.C., Fogg 1925.30.124.
Photo: The Fogg Art Museum, Harvard University, Cambridge.

16c. Bf. Panathenaic amphora: Ht. 82.7 cm., attributed to the Hobble Group, ca. 336 B.C., London B 608.
Photo: The British Museum, London.

16d. Bf. Panathenaic amphora: Ht. with lid 79 cm., without lid 61.9 cm., unattributed, Hellenistic, ca. 2nd. century B.C., Berlin VI. 4950.
Photo: Staatliche Museen Preussischer Kulturbesitz, Antikenabteilung, Berlin.

Figures

I

Introduction

THE FASCINATION OF GREEK POTTERY

Those who take time to do more than glance at specimens in museums find that ancient Greek pottery exerts a strange fascination.

The shapes are never purely decorative. Designed for specific use, they were used for that purpose, but despite their utilitarian character, the shapes are a source of wonder at the craftsman's skill. Whether sharply articulated or flowing smoothly from one part to the next, the lines are simple and pleasing to the eye. The symmetry is so remarkable, in fact, that a theory has been seriously proposed and skillfully documented to prove that they were designed and made according to geometric principles.[1] In fact, so conceived or not, no two vases are exactly alike, yet the illusion of planned geometric proportions is there.

The painting itself is fascinating, whether in the stern, strangely forceful black-figure technique, or in the graceful, human, yet idealized red-figure technique. The scenes, in their sharp depictions of myth or daily life, bring us close to the ancient world. Since murals and paintings on wood or other less durable fabrics for the most part have been destroyed, vase paintings provide some of our best illustrations of the Greek gods, heroes, and mythological creatures as envisioned by them. They show us life on the street and in the home, athletic events, armor, dress, and customs in a way that no written word can convey. They provide clues as to the use of implements and how things were made and done. Inscriptions of potters' and painters' names, favorites of the times, titles and

1

greetings to the holders of the vase— all add a special flavor. In brief, the vase paintings give substance to the words of literature and history.

Certain features of Greek vase painting are also of interest as reflections of ancient Greek thought. Perhaps the most obvious is the Greek love of symmetry so evident in architecture, but not more so than in the perfect symmetry of the Greek vase. Simplicity also is clearly expressed in the shape and painting of these vases. Attention is centered on the main figures — the humans, heroes, or gods involved.

The best of the Greek vase painters tended to concentrate on one or at most a very few figures. Even as the opening scene of the *Iliad* centers attention on the quarrel of Achilles with Agamemnon, so the master vase painters fixed upon the central issues.[2] The best black-figure artists, whether painting in narrative style, or depicting a single dramatic incident, concentrated on key figures and actions. Similarly, the masters of the red-figure technique presented single incidents from the myths or from everyday life.

During the Archaic and Classical periods the artist, like the philosopher and the dramatist, used events to present what he regarded as of real significance. He was "not trying to give a representative picture of life, but to express one conception as forcibly and as clearly"[3] as he could. The result was logical and taut. Typical also of ancient Greek thought was the artist's effort to portray not an individual, but the perfect representation of *The Athlete* or *The God*. The result was an expression of the ideal in human beauty.

Greek vase painting is interesting also for what it does not do. Scenes are impersonal; there are no portraits of individuals. It is notable for its paucity of background; buildings, trees, and other features are shown only when absolutely necessary; landscape scenes are not found. Decoration solely for the sake of decoration is not a feature of the main panels of Archaic or Classical vases. Only later, in Hellenistic times, is there pure decoration.

Initially, perhaps, the fascination of Attic black-figured pottery derives from its impact on the eye. A little study adds to its interest, revealing a picture record of the effects of diverse influences on its development. Special enjoyment is added as the personalities of its potters and painters emerge.

Perhaps the most striking feature of Attic black-figured work is the color scheme: black for humans, animals, and plant forms, and orange-red for the background; yet closer examination reveals that, though the colors are contrary to nature, the depictions are extremely lifelike. Immediately impressive too, is the severity of the technique in its use of black silhouette and incision. The general effect also is distinctive; normally, the subjects portrayed are austere, dignified, sombre, or even grim, though there are charmingly gay and even ribald exceptions.

During the century and a half of its existence (from late in the seventh century to about 450 B.C.) as a major vase painting technique, Attic black-figure was subjected to influences from outside and from within Attic workshops which determined its development. Also during these years, Attic black-figure painting underwent various modifications with regard to style, concepts of composition, themes portrayed, and conventions employed in their depiction.

The Attic black-figure technique originated when Proto-Attic artists began to employ influences from Corinth and when Athenian workshops began to develop new and better colors. Thus, the very earliest Attic black-figure painting is characterized by largeness and looseness of style inherited from the Proto-Attic tradition, but with influences from Corinth particularly evident in use of the black silhouette and an *Animal style* of painting. Much use was made of incision and of the colors red and white, also from Corinth, along with a newly developed orange-red for background. A little later, Athenian artists abandoned the large loose style of painting and adopted small animal friezes on small pots, as employed in Corinth.

In the course of time, however, Athenian artists threw off the Corinthian influence and developed a truly *Attic Human style* of painting on pots and cups of their own design. This is the period of the great masters of the black-figure technique. The development, about 530 B.C., of a red-figure technique in Attic workshops constituted the final major influence on the black-figure technique. It also heralded its eventual doom.

Concepts of *composition* changed with each new influence and the emergence of each new generation of painters. The earliest black-figured works, as might be expected, were large and were done on large pots in the Proto-Attic tradition. A little later, as Corinthian influence grew, small compositions crowded into bands and friezes became the norm. As the technique began to reach maturity and to throw off the Corinthian influence, painters sought new concepts of composition. Some drew elegant miniatures on large and small pots and on cups, sometimes depicting complex scenes in a narrative style. Others painted monumental compositions on large pots. Gradually, however, composition on better works tended to show a single scene with a very few characters and to emphasize mood. During the late stages of the black-figure technique, compositions often became crowded with figures, vines, and leaves or fussy in detail, as black-figure artists sought means to meet the challenge of the red-figure technique. Finally, composition degenerated along with painting as the better artists turned to the new technique.

Themes employed for the main scenes also changed with the passage of time. At first, animals and fantastic creatures tended to predominate. Later, the main scenes usually were mythological, showing the gods, heroes, and creatures of already ancient legends. Still later, after about 530 B.C., painters were inclined to portray more of everyday life, though heroic scenes continued to persist. In its final decline, black-figure scenes often were devoid of much meaning.

Interestingly, *conventions,* once developed (with respect to depiction of the human body, eyes, and drapery, and the use of different colors for male and female flesh) were more resistant to change. In this respect, black-figure differs in its development from the red-figure technique. In the latter, changes in the portrayal of eyes, hair, the human body, and drapery typify succeeding stages in the development of the technique. In black-figure, differences in the depiction of humans and their dress appear to arise more from each artist's whims than from changes in fashions or styles or portrayal. Not until the introduction of the red-figure technique did the old conventions begin to weaken. At this point, efforts were made to render the human form as well as the fall and folds of drapery more convincingly. In this effort, the black-figure technique failed to meet the challenge of the red-figure technique.

DATING OF POTTERY[4]

Before proceeding further, a few words of explanation are in order concerning overlapping of dates for the various stages in the development of the black-figure technique, and concerning dating in general.

Overlapping of dates for various developmental stages is reasonable and necessary. Unlike some manufacturers of fine ceramics in recent times, the Greeks did not use marks denoting the date of their works. Potters and painters sometimes signed their works, but such signatures are relatively rare, and records of the time do not tell us when the potters lived. More important, the stages of development are defined in terms of style and technique, not in terms of years. Styles and techniques do not begin or end abruptly; the older merges into the new, or the older and the new coexist for a time until the new replaces the old. The work of an innovator is contemporary with the bulk of the older style, while the work of an artist clinging to old traditions lingers on into a time when the bulk of the work is in the newer style.

Various methods are employed to determine the age of Greek pottery. Relative age can be determined from advances in style and technique evidencing progress from less to more advanced and from such evidence as the location of finds in graves and undisturbed stratified deposits. While these factors may show clearly that one style, technique, or pot is older than another, they do not tell how much older nor the age of either. Establishment of actual dates is difficult and can only be done when pottery can be tied to some known historic date.

Prior to the fifth century B.C., this is often impossible. Those events which are dated fairly accurately often cannot be tied to pottery and even if they can be so linked, the tie is often loose. Thus, though the founding of the Panathenaic games in the 560s B.C. provides a clue for dating the earliest Panathenaic prize amphorae, the actual date assigned to the first of these prizes varies by several years. By the end of the sixth century, records and writings of Greek historians provide more accurate historical dates, and from these, dating of pottery becomes more certain. The Athenian mound at Marathon has provided examples of pottery in use in 490 B.C., while the sack of Athens by the Persians in 480 B.C. provides a *terminus ante quem* for debris found at the foot of the Acropolis.

As is evident from the foregoing, specific dates assigned to a specific vase, painter, or potter should be viewed with caution. I have employed dates, because the amateur usually likes to have a frame of reference in fairly absolute terms. In this respect, I have indicated dates whenever feasible in the sense of rather general acceptance; otherwise, I have used half and quarter centuries.

INSCRIPTIONS[5]

Various inscriptions are found "painted" on Attic black-figured pottery. These include:

1. Letters strung together which have no meaning: Such inscriptions are often found on Tyrrhenian amphorae, where they appear to form part of the decoration.

2. Titles identifying the persons or other objects shown on the pot: Kleitias' meticulous identification of those shown on the François Vase (Florence 4209) is an outstanding example.

3. Titles explaining the subject: The phrase "the Games in honor of Patroklos," on a fragment of a dinos by Sophilos (Athens 15499) is an example. (This type of inscription is extremely rare.)

4. The words of a character shown on the pot: Achilles says "four" and Ajax "three" on an amphora (Vatican 334) by Exekias as the two are depicted playing dice.

5. Greetings to the holder of the item (usually a cup): "Hail and drink" on a lip-cup by the Phrynos Painter (Vatican 317) is typical.

6. Love names: The inscription *Stēsias kalos* on an amphora (Louvre F 53), potted by Exekias and decorated by a member of Group E, is the oldest such inscription yet found. The names of boys followed by *kalos* or of girls (far less often) followed by *kalé*, means "_____ is beautiful" (or fair). Such phrases did not refer to any figure painted on the pot, but rather to favorites of the time.

7. Signatures of potters and painters: Potters sometimes inscribed their pots "_____ *epoiesen*" or "_____ *epoiei*" (_____ made it); or "_____ *mepoiesen*" (_____ made me). Painters signed "_____ *egrapsen*" or "_____ *egrapse*" (_____ decorated it); or "_____ *megrapsen*" (_____ decorated me). Occasionally, the same person was both potter and painter and signed "_____ *egrapse kapoiese*" (_____ decorated and made it).[6]

8. Patronymics: Painters and potters sometimes added their father's name. Thus, a potter of many lip-cups and band-cups signed as "Tleson, son of Nearchos."

9. Panathenaic prize amphora inscriptions: The phrase "from the games at Athens" appeared regularly on prize amphorae donated at the Panathenaic games and early in the fourth century B.C., the names of archons were also shown.

In addition to inscriptions listed above, there were others made before firing of the pot, which are far more rare. Still other inscriptions were added after firing.

With the exception of the Panathenaic inscriptions, they were written forwards or backwards and at any angle that suited the painter.

PAINTERS' AND POTTERS' NAMES

About 350 black-figure painters and groups have been identified and given names, if the painter's name was not already known from his signature.[7] In addition, there were many painters and potters whose names are not known from signature and whose works have not been identified by special names. In all, potters and painters working in the black-figure technique between the end of the seventh century and the middle of the fifth century B.C. number in the hundreds. Among these only a few signed their works and even then, they were not consistent.[8] The best painters and potters sometimes failed to sign any of their works. Even when potters or painters signed, they often did not sign their best works.

There are only fifty-five sure complete signatures by potters[9] and sixteen or seventeen by painters (even if red-figure painters with only one black-figured item are included).

Among potters' signatures only three or four appear to belong to the early black-figure period; thirty-six fall into the mature period and only seven potters appear to have signed their work in the late black-figure period.

Most of the true black-figure painters' signatures appear in the mature black-figure period, as may be seen from the following list.

IDENTIFIED PAINTERS' SIGNATURES

Earliest Black-figure ca. 625-600 B.C.
  None.

Early Black-figure ca. 610-550 B.C.
  Sophilos

Mature Black-figure ca. 570-525 B.C.

Exekias	Nearchos
Kleitias	Sakonides
Lydos	

Late Black-figure ca. 530-450 B.C.

Douris*	Oltos*
Epiktetos*	Oikopheles
Epiktetos (II) —	Paideros
the Kleophrades	
Painter*	Paseas**
Euphiletos**	Psiax
Euphronios***	Skythes*

---

*Primarily red-figure painters, who did some black-figure work.
**Signature as painter not sure.
***Included here for his one Panathenaic amphora.

Painters whose names are not known from their signature have been given names by archaeologists based on a variety of factors such as:

1. The potter with whom the painter worked (e.g., the Amasis Painter).
2. A *kalos* name used (e.g., the Antimenes Painter).
3. The location of their first identified, discovered, or most famous work (e.g., the Rycroft Painter, named for his amphora which was once in the Rycroft collection).
4. A character depicted on one or more of their works (e.g., the Nettos Painter).
5. Stylistic characteristics of the painter (e.g., the C Painter — C for Corinthianizing).
6. The museum number assigned to one of the painter's items (e.g., the Painter of Acropolis 606).
7. The name of the former owner of the item, an archaeologist, etc. (e.g., the Beaune Painter).
8. The name of the dedicator of an item (e.g., the Epignote Painter).
9. Contractions of names (e.g., the Goltyr Painter — contraction of Goluchow-Tyrrhenian).

Potters, unfortunately, and probably for good reason, do not appear to have been as carefully studied as painters and have not been given names in the same way as painters. Only a few appear to be strongly distinctive — Nikosthenes and Pamphaios are exceptions — neither appears to have had pupils who adopted their styles.

ESSENTIAL ELEMENTS OF THE ATTIC BLACK-FIGURE TECHNIQUE[10]

In its perfected form, the Attic black-figure technique involved *silhouette drawing, incision*[11], and the use of four colors: the *orange* of the background, the *black* of the silhouettes, *white*, and *red* in various shades.[12]

Incision appeared in Attic pottery soon after the beginning of the seventh century B.C., but its use was not widespread until the middle of that century. It was employed to mark details such as strands of hair and beard, muscles, the eye, and other features which could be expressed by a line.

Red did not appear in Athenian pottery until the third quarter of that century, thereafter being used for subsidiary features, including men's faces (often purple), fillets, wreaths, and inscriptions.

White had become popular in Athens during the seventh century and was used widely for the flesh of females, the hair and beards of old men and, occasionally, for other features.

Incision, the reds and white all were borrowed from Corinth during the seventh century. The fine black of the figures and the oranges of the background were Attic in origin, but were not developed until about the end of the seventh century and not in perfected form until about 580 B.C.[13]

COLORS[14]

The major colors of the black-figure technique, the *black* used for the silhouette figures and the *orange-reds* of the background as well as the subsidiary *reds* and *white* warrant some explanation.

For centuries, the techniques by which the ancient Greeks produced the enduring colors of their black-figured (and red-figured) pottery remained a mystery. All efforts to reproduce the shiny blacks and orange-reds failed. For want of better explanations, the sheen was described as a varnish or a glaze and the blacks and orange-reds were called paints. It is now evident that color pigments were not employed to produce either color and that the pots were not coated with a true glaze. The colors, the sheen, and the ability of both to endure for more than 2,000 years, is explained by the skill of the ancient potters in utilizing the chemical and physical properties of their native clay.[15]

The Major Colors: Orange-red and Black

Chemical Properties

Due to the presence of ferric oxide, Attic clay in its natural state is a rich reddish-brown color. It fires to a yellow-brownish-red in an *oxidizing fire* (with the stoke hole of the kiln open to admit air). In a *reducing fire* the clay turns black. With the stoke hole closed, shutting off the supply of oxygen, carbon monoxide is formed, which absorbs oxygen from the ferric oxide producing black ferrous oxide. The chemical formula for this reaction is: $Fe_2O_3 + CO = 2FeO + CO_2$. The presence of water, from damp fuel, for example, results in a blacker magnetic oxide of iron, the reaction being: $3Fe_2O_3 + CO = 2Fe_3O_4 + CO_2$. If fired again in an *oxidizing fire,* the chemical processes are reversed, turning the clay back to the red ferric oxide. This property of Attic clay enabled the ancient potters to fire their pots either black or red.

To produce a pot with both red and black according to plan, the one for background and the other for figures and designs, constituted a unique achievement of the ancient Greeks. Their answer to the problem was found in preparing a concentrated solution of the same clay as that from which the pot was made. This concentrated solution was of such extremely fine particles as to constitute a colloidal suspension. A peptizing or deflocculating agent (such as potash) was added to the solution to prevent coagulation. Apparently no protective colloid (such as humin) actually was added to prevent recoagulation, though this has been suggested in the past. Aside from a somewhat higher percentage of ferric oxide in the concentrated solution, it did not materially differ chemically from the clay of the pot. The higher relative amount of ferric oxide in the concentrated solution probably was due to the elimination of heavier non-ferric oxides by the process of sedimentation. Because of its higher percentage of ferric oxide, the concentrated solution fired more intensely black or red than the mass of the clay.

Decorating the pot consisted of covering the entire surface of the vessel as it rotated on the wheel with a wash composed of yellow ochre, a natural iron oxide, sometimes mixed with a slight amount of a dilute version of the concentrated solution.[16] In the black-figure technique, figures were drawn on the pot and filled in with the strong concentration of the clay solution. Details were then incised with a sharp point. (In the red-figure technique, the background was filled with the concentrated solution, and the figures left reserved in the ochre wash, while details were drawn in with a dilute clay solution which fired brownish and by extruding a fine relief line of the concentrated solution.)[17]

The pot at this point, prior to firing, was brownish-red, varying only in tone as between the areas "painted" with the concentrated solution and the areas covered simply by the ochre wash — the areas with the concentrated solution being redder than the washed areas.

An initial oxidizing stage of firing, with heats up to 800° C., was necessary for good firing of the pot. This turned it red; the painted areas, however, were a deeper red and were shinier than the rest of the pot. The reducing stage which followed, with the heat increasing from 800° C. to about 945° C., turned the entire pot black. Again, the areas painted with the concentrated solution were darker and shinier than the unpainted areas. Cooling of the kiln at this point to about 900° C. was followed by the crucial third stage of reoxidizing with the kiln held at 900° C. and then gradually allowed to cool. In this stage, the unpainted areas covered only with the ochre wash returned to the red of ferric oxide, while the areas painted with the concentrated solution remained black.

Physical Properties

Various physical factors accounted for the sheen of the colors and for the fact that the areas painted with the concentrated clay solution remained black during the reoxidizing stage of firing.

Attic clay, and consequently the concentrated clay solution prepared by the Greek potters, contains illite and silica (in the form of celadonite). Particles of illite have a plate-like structure and, with evaporation and burnishing, tend to align themselves in a laminated layer along the plane of any surface to which they are applied. The smaller the particle sizes, the better they align in uniform layers, so producing a smooth surface with a high luster.

In addition, at temperatures ranging from 825° C. to 945° C., illite and silica enter a transitional stage known as sintering, which is short of melting, but in which the silica either forms new crystals or adds to existing crystals. This crystallization contributes to the creation of a glassy surface. These physical properties of illite and silica, plus care in producing a colloidal concentration of the clay and thorough burnishing prior to firing, enabled the potters to produce a high sheen on the black areas of their pottery. The fact that an ochre wash burnished and polished prior to firing remains shiny after firing enabled them to obtain a sheen on the red portions of pottery.

Nucleation of new silica crystals by sintering permits engulfment of other minerals which may be present. Once these crystals are formed, the engulfed mineral is cut off from chemical action by the atmosphere unless the quartz is heated to 1050° C., at which point it begins to melt readmitting contact with the air.

In the firing of their pots, the ancient Greek potters heated their kilns to the critical point of 945° C. only in the reducing stage during which the red ferric oxide was chemically changed to the black of ferrous oxide or magnetic oxide of iron. When the illite and silica sintered, the new crystals engulfed the black iron oxides in a dense quartz layer, which sealed them off from further contact with oxygen. In the subsequent reoxidizing stage of firing at heats ranging down from 900° C. to room temperature, oxygen was not able to penetrate the quartz layer to reoxidize the iron oxides. The clay of the pot, because it was composed of fine, but nowhere near colloidal-sized particles, did not sinter and remained porous. As a result, the oxygen easily penetrated unpainted sections and areas covered only by the ochre wash. The result was that the painted areas came out a shiny black, unpainted sections came out red, and areas with the ochre wash came out with an intensified red.

In order not to have the black blur into the red, painters using the black-figure technique first painted the figure contour and then filled it in (red-figure painters outlined the figures with a broad band of the concentrated solution — the so-called "eighth-inch" stripe — before filling in the rest of the background). The objective was to ensure that the line between figure and background was sharply marked by a thick layer.

Other Colors

Other colors, including white, purple, and special reds, were obtained by the use of white clay and a red oxide of iron pigment, alone or in combination with the normal concentrated clay solution.

White came from a very fine primary clay — a residual clay formed by the disintegration of feldspar unmoved by water, wind, or glacier. As it contained only a very slight admixture of iron, it fired white with a faint yellow tone. In the black-figure technique, white was used for the flesh of women, shield devices, clothing, furniture, and the hair and beards of old men. White also was employed as a white ground on the insides of cups, on the outsides of lekythoi and sometimes on other forms such as oinochoai. It could be burnished to a glossy white or left matte white. If white was used over black, it often flaked off or rubbed off leaving a dull black beneath.

A yellow, which actually is a beige or ivory, occasionally was used on black-figured skyphoi. This was made by adding 25% of the normal concentrated solution to the white slip.

Reds ranging from pale violet to purples and deep claret were used for men's beards and faces, clothing, wreaths, fillets, sashes, blood, shield devices, eyes, inscriptions, and tongue patterns. These reds were made of various combinations of a red oxide of iron, water, and about 10% of the concentrated clay solution. When used for the tongue pattern or on necks of vessels, they were applied directly on the clay body; sometimes they were painted over white. The reds held better when painted over the concentrated solution than when painted over the clay ground or over white. (White was not put on top of the reds.)

Pink, produced by adding 25% of the red mixture to the white slip, was used occasionally.

Gray was made by adding 5 to 25% of white slip to the normal concentrated clay solution.

THE SIX'S TECHNIQUE[18]

The Six's technique, which is mentioned from time to time in the following pages, needs a word of explanation. It was a method of adding white, pink, and red pictures to a pot, which previously had been covered entirely with a coat of the concentrated solution. Details and sometimes other figures were added by incision and the pot was then subjected to the usual three stages of firing.

BLACK-FIGURE ON WHITE BACKGROUND

Black-figure, as its name implies, involved painting of figures and designs in black against a light background. For the vast majority of black-figured works this meant painting against an orange or orange-red background. From the late sixth century on, however, black figures and designs occasionally were applied against a white background.

This type of work appears to be a minor variant of the black-figure technique and most authors merely note its existence in describing the development of the mid-fifth century white-ground lekythoi.[19] Interesting features of the white background work in black-figure are: (1) that portions of the pot were covered by a white slip or engobe prior to painting the black silhouette and, (2) on the best products, incision was made only to the depth of the underlying white; otherwise, the painting was the same as used in the black-figure technique.

During the late sixth century, work against white background sometimes was very carefully executed with superior draftsmanship to produce an impression of elegance. As a result, these pots enjoyed a certain deserved popularity. Production included lekythoi, oinochoai, pyxides, alabastra, and the insides of cups. Made for limited purposes, and probably expensive, they were comparatively rare. The better products were doubtless objects of pride in the home.[20]

With the decline of black-figure during the first half of the fifth century, work on white background also degenerated. Sometimes the black silhouette was replaced by semi-outline (partly outline, partly silhouette) and by outline drawing, while both pots and painting declined in quality.[21]

Notes on I — Introduction

1. Jay Hambidge, *Dynamic Symmetry – The Greek Vase* (New Haven: Yale University Press, 1948) and G. Caskey, *Geometry of Greek Vases* (Boston: Museum of Fine Arts, 1922).
2. H.D.F. Kitto, *The Greeks* (Baltimore: Penguin Books, Inc., 1965), p. 52.
3. Ibid., p. 184.
4. For more complete discussions of dating and chronology, see R.M. Cook, *Greek Painted Pottery,* (London: Methuen and Co., Ltd., 1960), pp. 261-75 (hereafter cited as *Greek P.P.*); and Joseph Veach Noble, *The Techniques of Attic Painted Pottery* (New York: Watson-Guptill Publishers in cooperation with the Metropolitan Museum of Art, 1965), pp. 87-9 (hereafter cited as *Attic P.P.*).
5. For additional details on inscriptions, see Cook, *Greek P.P.*, pp. 253-60; Noble, *Attic P.P.,* pp.xiii and 68; Gisela M.A. Richter, *Attic Red-figured Vases, A Survey* (New Haven: Yale University Press, 1958) rev. ed., pp. 14-21; idem, *A Handbook of Greek Art* (London: The Phaidon Press, 1960), rev. ed., pp. 314-16.
6. There is some controversy among scholars as to the meaning of *epoiesen,* with some asserting that it means both making and painting; I have followed the more generally accepted interpretation.
7. Based on the following: Sir John Davidson Beazley, *Attic Black-figure Vase Painters* (Oxford: Clarendon Press, 1956, hereafter cited as *ABV*); idem, *Paralipomena: Additions to Attic Black-figure Vase Painters and to Attic Red-figure Vase Painters* (Oxford: Clarendon Press, 1971), 2nd ed.; C.H.E. Haspels, *Attic Black-figured Lekythoi* (Paris: E. de Boccard, 1936) 2 vols.; and Dietrich von Bothmer, "The Painters of Tyrrhenian Vases," *American Journal Archaeology,* vol. 48, no. 2 (1944).
8. Noble, *Attic P.P.,* p.xii.
9. See Appendix II.
10. I have adopted Sir John Davidson Beazley's definition in this respect, and this section is based on *The Development of Attic Black-figure,* Sather Classical Lectures, vol. 24, 1951, (Berkeley and Los Angeles: University of California Press; London: Cambridge University Press, 1951) p. 1 (hereafter cited as *Dev.*).
11. Engraving with a sharp point. For a discussion of incision, see Noble, *Attic P.P.,* pp. 65-6.
12. Vases in which the red and/or white are omitted may still properly be called black-figure.
13. R. M. Cook, *The Greeks Till Alexander* (London: Thames and Hudson, 1961), pp. 44 and 94; also Cook, *Greek P.P.,* p. 90. The black actually was the same as

that used in the Geometric period, but was greatly refined and improved. Richter, *Red-figured Vases,* p. 28.

14. This section was prepared with the assistance of Joseph Veach Noble.

15. Credit for solving the mystery of the "painting" on ancient Greek pottery must be given to Dr. Theodor Schumann ("Oberflächenverzierung in der antiken Töpferkunst terra sigillata und griechische Schwartzrotmalerei," *Berichte der deutschen Keramischen Gesellschaft,* 23 [1942], pp. 408-26. This was summarized by Carl Weickert in "Zur Technik der griechischen Vasenmalerei," *Arch. Anzeiger* (1942), cols. 512-28. Neither of these articles was available outside of Europe until 1945. Schumann's work was carried on by Adam Winter and published in a series of articles in 1956-57 in the *Keramische Zeitschrift.* Further work and the most complete and readable account of Greek painting techniques is in Noble's *Attic P.P.*

16. Prior to the second generation of black-figure painters, the entire surface of the pot was simply smoothed and burnished; throughout the periods of the black-figure and red-figure techniques very small crude pots were made without the ochre wash.

17. The relief line was invented shortly after the middle of the sixth century B.C. by an Athenian potter or painter. See Noble, *Attic P.P.,* pp. 56-8 for a discussion of the relief line and how it was made.

18. Ibid., p. 66.

19. By convention, the term "white-ground" is used only for the red-figure technique white background vases, and is not used for work in the black-figure technique. Cook, *Greek P.P.,* p. 178.

20. Raymond V. Schoder, *Masterpieces of Greek Art* (London: Studio Books), commentary on plate 18.

21. Black-figure and semi-outline white-slipped lekythoi have been found in notable quantities in southern Italy and in Sicily and at one time were known as "Locrian" vases. See Cook, *Greek P.P.,* p. 326.

II

Characteristic Shapes

GENERAL

The proliferation of shapes which occurred in Attica from the late seventh century onward provides a useful key to the development of Attic black-figured pottery, since the introduction of new shapes and the disappearance of old shapes or their modification provide milestones of progress.

Among the first new items to appear in Attic black-figured pottery was the one-piece amphora, introduced as painted pottery in the late seventh century.[1] During the first half of the sixth century, many of these one-piece amphorae were decorated with a single panel on each side containing the head of a horse, man, or woman. Others were decorated in one piece (i.e., all around the pot). About 600 B.C., the olpe appeared in Attic pottery and, at about the same time, the dinos (or lebes) began to replace the much older kotyle-krater. Borrowings from Corinth in the early sixth century included the lekanis, plate, alabastron, aryballos, pyxis, column-krater, lekythos (with round or oval body), and the hydria. At first, these were adopted in uncritical acceptance of the Corinthian shapes, but sooner or later each was modified by Attic potters. The stumpy hydria used by the Polos Painter and his group at the beginning of the sixth century without change, for example, was given a flatter shoulder by mid-sixth century and by the last quarter of the century had become much slimmer with an even more angular shoulder[2] (compare Plate 2c with Plates 11a, b, and d).

16

Somewhere around 585 B.C., the first of the Komast cups appeared, again a Corinthian shape; these continued in vogue until about 570 B.C. Siana cups, an Attic shape, overlapped the Komasts, appearing about 575 B.C.; these endured in style until mid-century. These same years saw production of the Tyrrhenian amphorae. The first known Attic volute-krater is the famous Francqis Vase, made by Ergotimos and painted by Kleitias about 570 B.C.[3] The first Panathenaic amphora was also produced sometime between 570 and 560 B.C. Also, somewhere around the middle of the second quarter of the sixth century, the shoulder lekythos was developed. By 565 B.C., the first of the Little Master lip-cups had appeared with band-cups following some fifteen years later; the former continued in popularity until about 535 B.C., while the latter went on until at least 520 B.C. About the time lip-cups were dying out, the first Type A cups appeared, continuing in production in black-figure and red-figure through the end of the sixth century.

During the third quarter of the sixth century, the one-piece amphora had undergone various modifications and the calyx-krater may have been developed by Exekias.[4] In the fourth quarter of the sixth century, the Nikosthenic amphora and the cylindrical lekythos were developed in Attica. The latter shape continued with little change until just before mid-fifth century, when the "chimney" lekythos came into brief vogue among the last of the black-figured lekythoi.

Mention may be made of introduction of the pelike, stamnos, and kalpis at the end of the sixth century, though these items were painted primarily in the red-figure technique.

As noted in the introduction, all these shapes were utilitarian rather than purely decorative.

Necessity required large, coarse vessels with two vertical handles for handling, storage, and shipment of oil, olives, wine and grain; hence the *amphora* shape. Very large decorated amphorae were also used in the Geometric and Proto-Attic periods for funerary purposes and as grave markers. Geometric neck-amphorae of this type ranged up to more than five feet (ca. 160 cm.) in height; Proto-Attic neck-amphorae were sometimes taller than three feet. Fine painted amphorae of both the neck and one-piece types were used in the Archaic and Classical periods as decanters; the larger of these ranged around 18 inches (ca. 45 cm.) and the smaller around 12 inches (ca. 30 cm.) in height. Other amphorae, usually much larger, were given as prizes at festivals, as grave offerings, and for other special purposes; Panathenaic amphorae (normally, 25 to 35 inches or 63 to 89 cm. tall) and loutrophoroi (often 30 to 36 inches or 75 to 90 cm. tall) are typical of the latter uses.

The need for a vessel with two horizontal handles for carrying and a third vertical handle for dipping and pouring was met by development of the *hydria,* a pot ranging from 12 to 18 inches (ca. 30-45 cm.) tall. The pitcher or *oinochoe* was evolved for convenience in pouring small quantities of water or wine into bowls known as *kraters* or *dinoi* (also known as *lebetes*), which were used for mixing wine and water. Oinochoai varied widely in shape and size; the normal was from 6 to 12 inches (ca. 15 to 30 cm.) tall. The bowls ranged in height from 12 to 18 inches (30 to 45 cm.).

Kylikes or cups of various stemmed and unstemmed types, and *skyphoi* were used for drinking wine or wine mixed with water. The normal size for kylikes was from 8 to 14 inches (20 to 35 cm.) in diameter; some, including skyphoi were as small as 4 inches (ca. 10 cm.) across, while others were very large, ranging up to 22 or more inches (55 cm. plus) in diameter.[5]

Smaller vessels include a variety of shapes of which the more important may be mentioned. *Lekythoi* were designed to hold oil and unguents, but were often used later in offerings to the dead. Normally, these were from 6 to 10 inches (ca. 15 to 25 cm.) high, though they sometimes were as small as 3 inches (ca. 7.5 cm.) or as tall as 14 inches (ca. 35 cm.). *Pyxides,* round boxes of about 4 inches (ca. 10 cm.) in diameter, were used for cosmetics and trinkets. *Aryballoi* were oil bottles of from 2 to 6 inches (ca. 5 to 13 cm.) in height, used by athletes at their baths. *Alabastra* were perfume containers, 3 to 8 inches (ca. 7 to 20 cm.) high.

Each shape, though often beautifully decorated, thus had a specific use and was so used.

IMPORTANT SHAPES

Certain of the shapes mentioned above are sufficiently important, distinctive or characteristic of a particular period to warrant additional discussion and illustration.[6]

One-piece Amphorae

The one-piece amphora (usually referred to simply as the amphora) is so-called because the neck flows smoothly into the body, in contrast to the off-set neck of the neck-amphora.

The Type B (or Ia) one-piece amphora:[7]

This was introduced about 610 B.C., has a lip which is flaring and straight to slightly concave, plain round handles, and an inverted echinus foot in one degree.[8] Its prototype was a heavy sagging pot not unlike the later pelike. By 600 B.C., the belly had lifted to the middle of the body; later, it slimmed and became more delicate; still later, it developed a high belly.[9] The decoration normally was on two panels, one on the front and one on the reverse of the vase.

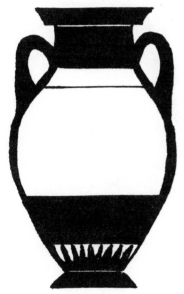

Fig. 1 Type B
One-piece Amphora

Fig. 2 Type A
One-piece Amphora

Type A (or Ib) one-piece amphora:

This appeared about 550 B.C., and is somewhat more elaborate than the older form, with a longer neck and shoulders, a less tense belly, flat flanged handles, foot in two degrees and a fillet between foot and base. The decoration, also on front and back panels, begins lower down than on Type B and the sides of the flanged handles are decorated with ivy leaves.

Type C (or Ic):

A third modification of the amphora, Type C (or Ic) became common especially in the third quarter of the sixth century (and continued in popularity with red-figure painters from 520 to 470 B.C.). Similar to Type B, this modification had, however, a convex slightly spreading mouth and either an inverted echinus or a torus foot.

Fig. 3 Type C
One-piece Amphora

Neck-Amphorae

The neck-amphora, which had been common in Protogeometric, Geometric, and Proto-Attic pottery, continued to be popular, although in much smaller versions, throughout the period of the black-figure technique.

Type A (or IIa):

Earlier examples of the Type A (or IIa) neck-amphora vary as to the shape of the foot and the mouth, but once the shape had evolved and become standardized, the lip was echinus-shaped and the foot torus.

One relatively large version of the neck-amphora, the so-called S.O.S. amphora, was a utilitarian pot, all black except for an S.O.S. pattern on the neck. It is of little importance, except that it was widely exported, presumably for its contents, and because it served as a prototype for the more interesting and smaller Tyrrhenian amphora.[10]

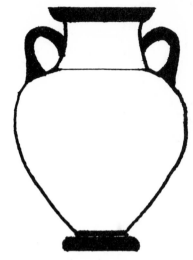

Fig. 4 Type A
Neck Amphora

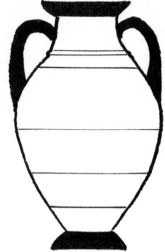

Fig. 5 Tyrrhenian
Neck Amphora

Tyrrhenian Amphorae:

The Tyrrhenian amphorae, produced during the second quarter of the sixth century, are so-called because most of them were found in the Etruscan area north of Rome, where they were once thought to have been made. Their shape is characterized by a thick squat neck, raised collar at the juncture of neck and body, a long egg-shaped body, and a spreading inverted echinus shaped foot. The neck decoration usually is a chain of lotus and palmettes or animals. The shoulder frieze often has human subjects such as battles, Amazonomachies, sacrifices, or departure scenes. Belly friezes below the main scene include bands of animals or sphinxes. At the base are rays. The draftsmanship is careless, rough, and hurried. The style often is pretentious and inferior, though sometimes it is vigorous and fresh. These amphorae are decorated in black against a reddish-tan clay background with purple and white over the black. Inscriptions, which litter the fields, often are nonsensical and sometimes are mere blobs that look like letters.

Nikosthenic Amphora:

The *Nikosthenic amphora* was a special type of neck-amphora produced in the workshop of the potter Nikosthenes during the late sixth century. Apparently a revised form of an Italian shape, it is characterized by a conical neck, which at its base is nearly as wide as the body and by broad, flat strap handles that join into the lip.

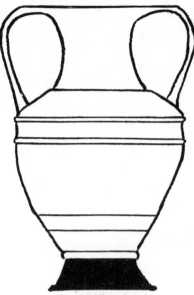

Fig. 6 Nikosthenic
Neck Amphora

Panathenaic Amphora:[11]

This was a special type of neck-amphora which appeared in the second quarter of the sixth century B.C. Filled with the famous Attic oil, amphorae of this type were awarded to winners of events at the quadrennial Panathenaic games at Athens in honor of the city's patron goddess. These amphorae continued to be awarded at the festivals into the second century B.C. Painted in the black-figure technique, they thus endured long after both black-figure and red-figure painting on other forms of pottery and as such, deserve rather detailed treatment.

True "prize amphorae" bore the inscription "from the games at Athens." In addition, however, numerous vases were of the same shape, often similar in size, and in the same style of decoration, but without the inscription; accordingly, fragmentary items often cannot be identified positively as prize amphorae. Others were of the same shape and size, but pictured no Panathenaic scenes, while still others were of much smaller size.

Athletic contests are believed to have been introduced at the Panathenaic Games in the year 566 B.C. Equestrian contests, however, appear to have been a part of the festival even earlier, so at least one vase, the Burgon Vase,[12] may slightly antedate this year.

Though the shape of the Panathenaic amphora underwent

changes, which at first made it stronger, more compact and handsomer, it then degenerated, although the basic shape was retained. Typically, it was a very large vase with a short, thin neck, a swelling body tapering sharply at the base and with a small foot.

Subjects portrayed also followed a uniform pattern.[13] On the obverse was Athena Promachos (armed and holding her spear aloft). On the reverse was a depiction of the event in which the winner had been successful. Interestingly, the reverse was always drawn in the natural style of the period in which it was painted; the obverse or Athena side was drawn in the natural contemporary manner throughout the Archaic period, but was done in traditional style thereafter, and so remained "archaic."

In the course of time, the shape, decoration, and, particularly, the depiction of Athena on the obverse underwent changes which help to date this long series of vases.

On the earliest Panathenaic amphora, the Burgon Vase, Athena is pictured as short and stout with both feet planted solidly on the ground. She is simply dressed in a peplos with no folds. Her helmet is a skull cap with an attached high crest. Her aegis is a short bib decorated with a snake. She faces to the left with the outside of her shield presented to the viewer. In succeeding years, shield devices varied, but the depiction remained much the same. During this early period, the vase itself was stout and squat with large handles and an inverted echinus foot, "a neater version of the old S.O.S. amphora."[14]

By 535-530 B.C., Athena was flanked left and right by columns topped with cocks. She appeared less stout and more energetic, with one heel raised from the ground. Instead of the simple peplos, she wore two garments, both with many folds. Her helmet was more complicated with a frontlet, neckpiece, and floral ornament. Her aegis was covered with scales and trimmed with serpents. Though shield devices continued to vary, the rim usually was red. A tongue pattern had appeared above Athena on the shoulder and a floral design had become standard on the neck. The vase shape was longer in body and shorter in neck (see Plates 15a, 15b, and 15c for typical Panathenaic amphorae of the last third of the sixth century B.C.).

During the last quarter of the sixth century, Athena began to wear a chiton in place of the peplos, in keeping with changing styles. Her figure also tended to become slimmer. Her shield device varied as each painter tended to confine himself to one design. Shield rims became black with red dots, instead of their previous red. Athena varied also in other details, but, in general, remained much the same in the succeeding years until the end of the fifth century. The vase shape became gradually stronger and more compact with a higher shoulder, more curved at shoulder and base, with the handles closer to the neck and with a torus foot replacing the inverted echinus foot.

In the late fifth century, there was a trend to make Athena thinner and thinner, until by 400 B.C. she was very lean with long legs, a long neck, and an absurdly small head. (See Plate 15d for an example attributed to the Kuban Group of about 400 B.C.) Her garments, meanwhile, lost their folds, though they became more and more floridly decorated. The cocks on the columns also degenerated in style. In the following ten years, these cocks disappeared altogether and were replaced thereafter by symbols, usually statuettes. Athena, however, recovered normal proportions during the same decade. During this period, the shape of the amphora had slackened, with incurve at shoulder and base increased. (See Plate 16a for a Panathenaic amphora of ca. 366 B.C. attributed to the Polyzelos Group.)

Introduction in the early fourth century of the names of the archon in office at the time the oil was collected constituted a major addition to the inscriptions on Panathenaic amphorae. An early fragment may bear the archon name Philokles of 392/1 B.C., but the first such name which can be restored with certainty is that of Hippodamos, who held office 375/4; the next is Asteios of 373/2, while the last archon's name to appear is that of Polemon, 312/11 B.C. During the first third of the fourth century, Athena was depicted in normal proportions; her drapery was plain, with simple folds, while her helmet crest gradually became more fanciful; otherwise, she underwent no major change. The vase, however, came to be made with a flaring lip, replacing the former echinus lip, with thinner handles and with a foot in two degrees.

By 363 B.C., artists were adding swallow tails to Athena's drapery and making her helmet crest even more fanciful.

A major change occurred sometime between 359 and 348 B.C., when Athena was faced to the right (instead of to the left as on all previous vases) and the inside of her shield was presented to the viewer (see Plate 16b for an example). Thereafter, the figure of Athena became almost stereotyped except for a brief period around 336 B.C. during which she was hampered by a "hobble skirt." (Plate 16c illustrates a Panathenaic amphora attributed to the Hobble Group.) Her skirt became longer, her garments clung closer to her body. Swallow-tails on her shoulder wraps were echoed on the lower edges of her outer garment above her knees and at her ankles to form a train. Her aegis was reduced to a mere cross cord with a small gorgoneion in the middle. The shape of the vase remained much the same.

In the following years, drawing gradually degenerated so that by the second century B.C., the goddess was thoroughly debased, wearing flowing drapery and a baroque Corinthian (instead of Attic) helmet (see Plate 16d for a Hellenistic Panathenaic amphora). Pot making similarly had declined as an art and the amphora was an ugly caricature of earlier shapes.

Kylikes or Cups[15]

Kylikes, perhaps even more than the various amphora types, exercised a special fascination for both potter and painter, with the result that there are numerous types and sub-types. To sharpen the distinctions between the main types, data on each is presented in outline form below.

Komast Cups (ca. 585-570 B.C.)

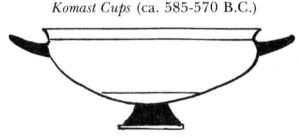

Figure 7   Komast Cup

LIP: The lip is short and offset, and decorated with incised rosettes or a rough net pattern.

BOWL: The bowl is rounded in shape. The decoration usually consists of three dancing male revelers, known as Komasts (see Plates 3b and 3c). At first, the Komasts were of special shape and wore padded chitons. Later they were naked, undeformed, and were sometimes joined by a short-skirted female. Purple is common for faces and chests. Under the handles are lotus flowers with sprawling tendrils.

HANDLES: Black.

JUNCTURE OF BOWL AND STEM : A sharp angle.

STEM: Black; conical and low.

FOOT: Flaring; black with a reserved edge.

INSIDE DECORATION: None (black).

OTHER COMMENTS: The Komast cups are named after the Komasts pictured on them. They have a casual, top-heavy look. The shape was borrowed from Corinth, where similar cups had been common since the early sixth century, but it was greatly modified by the Attic potters. The decoration was strongly influenced by Corinth.

Siana Cups (ca. 575-550 B.C.)

Figure 8 Siana Cup

LIP: The lip is offset and higher than on the Komast cups.

BOWL: The bowl is rounded, but wider than that of the Komast cup. The lower part of the bowl is usually black except for a narrow reserved strip two-thirds of the way up, though sometimes the lower part is elaborately decorated. There are two types of decoration:
(1) The "Double-decker" Type has one design on the lip, usually floral (ivy branches) or hounds coursing a hare, while another design of half-sized figures occupies the narrow handle zone; a narrow black line usually distinguishes the lip from the handle zone. Sometimes this type has a black lip.
(2) The "Overlap" Type has a decoration of riders, dinner parties, or battle scenes split into dueling pairs straddling both the handle and lip areas.

HANDLES: Black.

JUNCTURE OF BOWL AND STEM : A sharp angle.

STEM: Black; conical and higher than on the Komast cup.

FOOT: Flaring, black with a reserved edge.

INSIDE DECORATION: The inside of the cup usually contains a large tondo within a thick border, usually of tongues and bands of dots with the rest black except for a narrow reserved stripe near the edge of the lip. At first, the tondo consisted of a single running or flying figure, but later, two figures became common.

OTHER COMMENTS: Siana cups are named after two examples found at Siana on the island of Rhodes. The shape was developed by Attic potters. The cups were planned for a balance of light and dark; the decoration was strongly influenced by Corinth.

Contemporary with the Siana cups were the so-called *merrythought cups* named after the shape of their handles, which had knobs and so resembled wishbones. Unlike the other cups of the time, these cups had bowls shaped like a segment of a sphere with no offsetting of the lip. The foot and stem were taller than on the Siana cup. The shape never became popular.

Little Master Cups include two major varieties, the band-cup and the lip-cup with their variants. The former appeared a little earlier and died out a little sooner than the latter. Their general name derives from the fine miniaturist style of their decoration.

Lip-cups (ca. 565-535 B.C.)

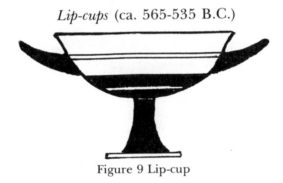

Figure 9 Lip-cup

LIP: The lip is slightly out-curved and clearly tooled off from the bowl. It is either reserved and blank or decorated with one or a very few human or animal figures.

BOWL: The shape of the bowl is spreading. The handle zone areas are reserved with an inscription of the potter's name or a salute to the drinker, or they are blank. Palmettes appear on each side of the handles. The lower bowl is black except for a narrow reserved striping, and a thin black line, set well below the lip, emphasizes the articulation between lip and bowl.

HANDLES: Black on the outside, but reserved on their inner faces.

JUNCTURE OF BOWL AND STEM : A sharp angle.

STEM: Tall and black.

FOOT: Black except for the edge which is reserved.

INSIDE DECORATION: Many of the cups are plain black except for a small reserved disc in the middle containing a circle and its center. Others have a tondo in the center. There is often a narrow reserved stripe near the rim.

OTHER COMMENTS: The cup is named from the offset lip. It gives the general impression of a light cup. The cup was developed by Attic painters and has very fine painting and incision.

Gordion Cups, so-called from the town in Phrygia where one was found, are an early type of lip-cup dating to the years 565-540. They differ from the usual lip-cup in several respects: (1) the inside has an elaborate tondo like the Siana cup; (2) the offset lip is black; (3) the foot is much lower than on the usual lip-cup; (4) the cup is smaller and of delicate fabric; (5) apart from palmettes at each side of the handles, the decoration consists only of potters' signatures in fine letters.

Band-cups (ca. 550-520 B.C.)

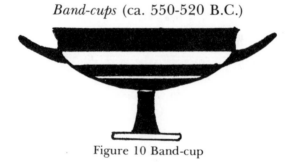

Figure 10 Band-cup

LIP: The lip passes into the bowl in a gradual curve, and is black.

BOWL: The shape is spreading. The handle zone is usually filled with many figures. There are neat palmettes at the handles, and the lower bowl is black.

HANDLES: Black.

JUNCTURE OF BOWL AND STEM : Sharp angle, often masked by a small red or purple fillet.

STEM: Tall and black.

FOOT: Black with reserved edge.

INSIDE DECORATION: Nearly all are plain black except for a small reserved disc in the middle containing a circle and its center.

OTHER COMMENTS: These cups are named after the band effect of the black lip, reserved handle zone, and black lower bowl. The general impression they give is of a dark cup. The shape is Attic and the painting is completely Attic. Incision is fine, but the technique is often poorer than on lip-cups.

Cassel cups are a small variety of the band-cup and are distinguished by the fact that the outside is entirely covered with bands of simple decoration. They date to the years 550-525 B.C.

Floral band-cups are another small variety of band-cups. They are characterized by a chain of palmettes along the handle frieze. A late variety, they date from about 540 to a little after 520 B.C.

Droop cups (ca. 560-510 B.C.)[16]

LIP: The lip passes smoothly into the bowl. The lip is black.

BOWL: The shape is spreading. The handle zone is decorated with a chain of buds; next below is a band often of upside-down silhouette animals or other figures. The base of the bowl is decorated with rays and is separated from the zone above by stripes.

HANDLES: Black.

JUNCTURE OF BOWL AND STEM : Sharp Angle.

STEM: Tall, reserved, often with broad unpainted channeling at the top.

FOOT: Convex with a black edge.

INSIDE DECORATION: There is a thin reserved band some distance below the top of the rim; sometimes the interior is decorated with a small medallion or with a central dot surrounded by a circle or two or else left entirely black.

OTHER COMMENTS: The cups were named after Professor J. P. Droop following his article in the *Journal of Hellenic Studies* in

1910, which contained a description of this type of cup. The cup has a balance of light and dark. The shape is Attic and the painting is entirely Attic.

In addition to the regular Droop cups, there are some late-comers (560-510 B.C.) in which the bowl was entirely covered with black.[17]

Eye or Type A or Type II Cups (ca. 535-500 B.C.)[18]

Figure 12 Eye-cup

(Note: The shape is Type A; only if the cup is decorated with "apotropaic" eyes is it properly called an eye-cup.)

LIP: The lip passes smoothly into the bowl.

BOWL: The bowl is a shallow single curve. The lip area and upper bowl are often decorated on each side with a pair of large apotropaic eyes with strong brows. Between the eyes is a rough nose or a figure or figures. At the handles are more figures or vines, and at the base of the bowl are bands or rays.

HANDLES: Black.

JUNCTURE OF BOWL AND STEM : Sharp angle, marked off by a thick fillet.

STEM: Black; short and stout.

FOOT: Deep, strongly modelled, black, reserved on the edge.

INSIDE DECORATION: A simple reserved circle or a shabby gorgone-ion in the center with the rest black.

OTHER COMMENTS: The appearance is of a light cup. The shape is Attic, as is the painting, though copied by others.

A few Type B (or Type III) cups and Type C cups also were painted in black-figure. The former was primarily a red-figure shape, while the latter seems never to have been very popular among better black-figure painters.

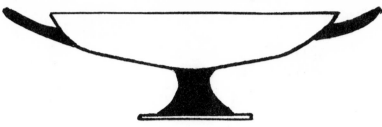

Fig. 13 Type B Cup

Fig. 14 Type C Cup

Lekythoi[19]

The lekythos deserves rather special mention because it became the chief shape for black-figure painters during the first half of the fifth century (and because it also was the primary shape employed for white-ground work by red-figure painters from about 460 B.C. until the end of the fifth century).

The first Attic lekythoi appeared early in the sixth century. Derived from Corinthian shapes, they are known as *Deianeiran lekythoi.* Two types of this early shape may be distinguished: the *round lekythos,* apparently derived from the aryballos, and the *elongated oval lekythos,* apparently derived from the alabastron. The former was much rarer than the latter, though neither became very popular.

In the course of the first half of the sixth century B.C., various sub-types of these round and oval lekythoi were developed, but without lasting result.

Sometime about 560 B.C., the shoulder lekythos was invented in an Attic workshop. This new form had a definite but rounded shoulder, a short neck ring and a mouth which was shorter than in the earlier types. The broad body tapered down to an inverted echinus foot.

Fig. 15 Deianeiran Lekythos,
Round

Figure 16 Deianeiran Lekythos,
Oval

Fig. 17 Early
Shoulder Lekythos

Fig. 18 Shoulder
Lekythos ca. 540-530 B.C.

Within twenty years, the drip ring had been eliminated in favor of a ridge where shoulder and neck met and the mouth had become echinus-shaped. The shoulders were widened and flattened; a red line marked the sharp division of the shoulder and body, while the broad body tapered down to an inverted echinus foot.

In succeeding years, the shape was slimmed down, the lip was altered to a cup shape and the foot to a torus shape, while a fillet often divided foot from base.

Fig. 19 Standard
Lekythos ca. 500 B.C.

Fig. 20 Chimney Lekythos
ca. 470 B.C.

By the end of the sixth century B.C., the standard form had been evolved with a long cylindrical body, round at the base and slightly convex just below the shoulder. The foot was either a simple torus shape or of two degrees, the upper straight-edged and reserved, the lower torus-shaped and black. Lip, handle, and lower body were black, leaving the shoulder and upper body free for decoration.

After about 470 BC., the "chimney" lekythos came into brief vogue for the last of the black-figure works, though many of the standard lekythoi continued to be used in smaller versions, while larger varieties were taken over by red-figure artists.

Other Shapes

On the following pages are shown a few of the more typical black-figure shapes not already discussed. Areas of the pots normally black are so shown and areas normally containing the orange-red background and the black silhouette figures and designs are left blank.

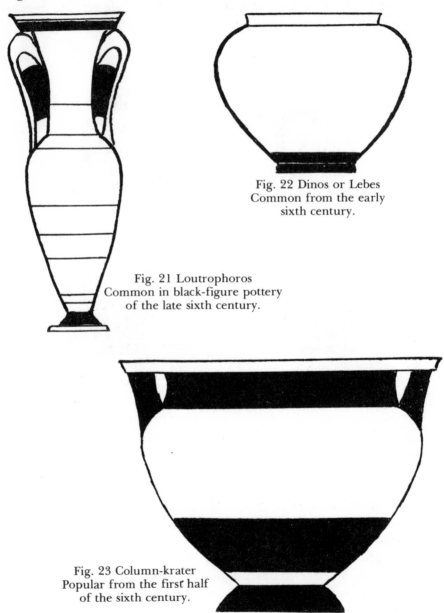

Fig. 22 Dinos or Lebes
Common from the early
sixth century.

Fig. 21 Loutrophoros
Common in black-figure pottery
of the late sixth century.

Fig. 23 Column-krater
Popular from the first half
of the sixth century.

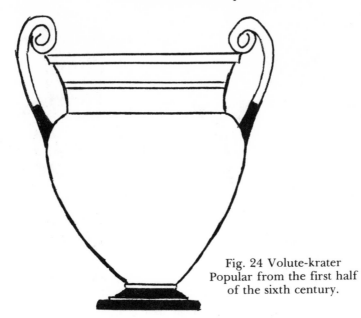

Fig. 24 Volute-krater
Popular from the first half
of the sixth century.

Fig. 25 Oinochoe
There were many types of
Oinochoai common through-
out the sixth century.

Fig. 26 Oinochoe

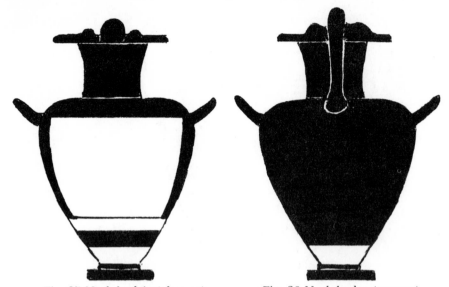

Fig. 27 Neck-hydria (obverse)   Fig. 28 Neck-hydria (reverse)

Prevalent during the sixth century.

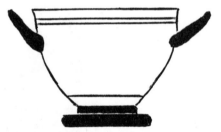

Fig. 29 Skyphos

Common throughout the sixth century.

POTTERS[20]

The complete signatures of about fifty-five potters have been found. In addition, there are some dozen signatures that may be those of potters or which are partial signatures. Twenty-six of the potters whose full name is known signed on only one of their known items, and seventeen others signed five or less of their known items. Even the outstanding potters appear to have signed few of their works.

On early black-figured work, potters' signatures are rare. None are found on Komast cups and on Siana cups only one signature each by Chieron and Taleides are known. No signatures are found on Tyrrhenian amphorae and on other pots there are only three signatures, all of Sophilos.

During the mature black-figure period, about thirty-four potters signed one or more of their known works; thirty of these signed lip, band, Gordion or Droop cups. Among the important potters of this period seven must be mentioned. The earliest, Ergotimos, was the master potter of the great volute krater known as the François Vase, painted by Kleitias. Ergotimos also signed six other known items including three Gordion cups. Other potters of Little Master and Droop cups include Tleson with about eighty-three signed cups, Hermogenes and Xenokles with about twenty-eight cups each, and Taleides with fifteen items.[21] Exekias, the greatest painter of the period, also is credited with twelve items as potter including four lip-cups, one Type A cup, a dinos, four amphorae of various types, and two other fragmentary items. The most prolific of all potters appears to have been Nikosthenes, with 125 signed works and fifty-four other items clearly potted by him though not signed. Most of these were his special type of neck-amphora, though he also potted many cups and some other items.

In the late black-figure period, the only potter of note is Pamphaios. Incidentally, he is the only potter to copy Nikosthenes. In black-figure, Pamphaios is credited with potting two hydria and eight cups. He went on to become a prominent potter of some forty items for red-figure painters.

REFERENCE TO ILLUSTRATIONS

In concluding this chapter, it appears useful to cite the numbers of the photographic plates at the back of this book which illustrate the various shapes described in the preceeding pages or mentioned hereafter.

SHAPE	PLATE
Geometric neck-amphora	1a
Proto-Attic neck-amphora	1b — 1d
One-piece amphorae	
Early Type B (panel)	4b
Type B	6a, 6d, 7a, 11c
Type A	7c, 10c, 11c
Type C	6b

SHAPE	PLATE
Neck amphorae	
Early	2a, 2b
Type A	7b, 7d
Type A (small)	12d
Tyrrhenian	4a
Nikosthenic	10b
Panathenaic	14d — 16d
Cups and Kylikes	
Komast cup	3b
Siana cup	3d
Lip-cup	8a, 8b
Band-cup	8c
Cassel cup	8d
Droop cup	9a
Proto-A cup	9b
Type A (or eye-cup)	9c
Type B	9d
Stemless	10a
Skyphos	3c, 13d
Loutrophoros	12a
Dinos	2d, 5b
Hydriai	
Early Corinthian type	2c
Neck-hydria (special)	6c
Neck-hydria	10d, 11a, 11b
Kraters	
Column-krater	5d
Volute-krater	5a
Oinochoe	12b
Lekythoi	
Oval lekythos	4c
Early shoulder lekythos	4d
Cylindrical, shoulder lekythos	12c, 13a — 13c, 14a, 14b
Chimney lekythos	14c

Notes on II — Characteristic Shapes

1. This shape is rare outside of Attic pottery. Cook, *Greek P.P.*, p. 222.
2. Ibid., pp. 77-8.
3. Beazley, *Dev.*, p. 26.
4. Ibid., p. 70 and idem, "Attic Black-figure: A sketch," *Proceedings of The British Academy*, vol. XIV (London: Humphrey Mulford Amen House, E.C.; Oxford: University of Oxford Press, 1930), p. 29.
5. The Type B cups mentioned later were often very large.
6. For more complete discussions of shapes, uses, names, and sizes, see Gisela M.A. Richter and Marjorie J. Milne, *Shapes and Names of Athenian Vases* (New York: The Metropolitan Museum of Art, 1935); Cook, *Greek P.P.*, pp. 217-41; Noble, *Attic P.P.*, pp. 11-30; and Folsom, *Handbook of Greek Pottery*, pp. 101-6 and 147-96.
7. Beazley, *Dev.*, and Cook, *Greek P.P.*, classify amphorae as Types A, B, and C; while Richter and Milne in *Shapes*, classify amphorae as Types 1a, 1b, 1c, etc.
8. See Appendix V for sketches of lips, feet, and handles.
9. Cook, *Greek P.P.*, p. 77.
10. Ibid, p. 76.
11. This section is based almost entirely on Beazley's *Dev.*, pp. 88-100. See also Cook, *Greek P.P.*, pp. 89-90 and 222; P.E. Arias and Max Hirmer, *A History of Greek Vase Painting* (London: Thames and Hudson, 1962), pp. 314-15.
12. So called for the scholar who found it, Beazley, *Dev.*, p. 88; see Plate 14d.
13. For painters of Panathenaic amphorae see Appendix IV.
14. Cook, *Greek P.P.*, p. 89.
15. For additional information on cups, see Cook, *Greek P.P.*, pp. 75-85, 169-70, and 236-37; Beazley, *Dev.*, pp. 20-5, 52-6, 62, and 67-8; Noble, *Attic P.P.*, pp. 20-1 and Plates 132-34; Arias and Hirmer, *Greek Vase Painting*, 293-95; and Richter and Milne, *Shapes*, pp. 24-5 and Figures 152-66.
16. See Cook, *Greek P.P.*, pp. 80-1; J.P. Droop, "The Dates of the Vases Called 'Cyrenaic'," *Journal of Hellenic Studies*, vol. 30 (1910), pp. 21-7; and P.N. Ure, "Droop Cups," *Journal of Hellenic Studies*, vol. 52, part 1 (1932).
17. Cook, *Greek P.P.*, p. 81.
18. Beazley and Cook use the terms Type A, B, and C for cups, while Richter and Milne employ the terms Type I, II, and III, with Type I including all the cups mentioned herein from the Komast cups through the Droop cups plus the Type C cup.
19. This section is based on Haspel's *Black-figured Lekythoi*.
20. This section is based on Appendix II of Beazley's *ABV*, as revised by his *Paralipomena*.
21. Including the Siana cup mentioned above, seven Little Master cups and seven other items.

III

Origins of Attic Black-Figure[1]

BACKGROUND: ELEVENTH TO SEVENTH CENTURY B.C.

Vase-making and painting of Attica may be traced back to the eleventh century B.C., when a Protogeometric style was developed in a clear break from the earlier Mycenaean style. Mycenaean pottery, in its decline during the eleventh century, had been characterized by slack, sagging shapes decorated with lifeless plant and animal forms, stylized almost beyond recognition, or simply with bands around the pot. Protogeometric pottery, on the other hand, was solid and strong; the painting was in sharp contrasts of black and light with large black areas. Heavy solid lines and bands encircled the pots with concentric circles and semicircles relieving the horizontal effect.

Protogeometric pottery merged gradually into the Geometric in the tenth century B.C. Geometric vases were firm, taut vessels painted with geometric designs of hatched meanders and swastikas, cross-hatched triangles and lozenges, lines, and panels. Animals and humans occupied little space and, when shown, were angular silhouettes.

As trade and communications with the East developed in the last half of the eighth century, oriental art styles found their way to Greece. Especially in Corinth, this orientalizing influence with its animals, plant forms, and flowing lines found ready acceptance. A silhouette black-figure Animal style of vase painting developed there and dominated the Greek market from about 725 to 550 B.C. This black silhouette style featured lions, panthers, sirens, griffins, various winged animals, and other fantastic creatures as the main subjects, with rosettes as the chief items of subsidiary design.

In other areas, including Laconia, the Cycladic Islands, and East Greek centers, other black-figure and semi-black-figure or semi-outline schools developed as they turned from the Geometric tradition to acceptance of orientalizing influences.

EARLY PROTO-ATTIC AND BLACK AND WHITE STYLE

In Attica, the break with the Geometric style led to development of a style featuring outline drawing called Proto-Attic somewhat inappropriately (since it certainly was not the first Attic style). Why outline drawing should have been adopted is not clear. Figures of animals and birds usually had been silhouette and figures of humans always had been silhouette in the Geometric period. The break with the Geometric style was slow, and items painted in the transition period often are difficult to classify conclusively. Gradually, in the years 710 to 680 B.C., as the orientalizing influence with its new motifs and flowing lines mixed with the Geometric tradition, a distinctive Proto-Attic style was created.[2] The succeeding years, 680 to 650 B.C., saw the rapid development and decline of a *Black and White style,* fully free of the Geometric tradition.[3] This was an outline style of broad contrasts between black and white in which each had about equal value. It was turbulent and impatient, and generous use was made of incision and of a yellowish white for the flesh of both males and females.

A few painters and their works may be mentioned to illustrate the transition from the older Geometric style to the early Proto-Attic and, subsequently, to its full flowering in the Black and White style.

The *Analatos Painter* is one of the first Proto-Attic painters whose work can be distinguished. A hydria, found at Analatos in Attica (Athens N.M. 2696) from which he derives his sobriquet, probably was painted in the closing years of the eighth century.[4] This vase illustrates the break with the Geometric tradition. The dancing men and women on the neck of the pot, though clearly derived from Geometric predecessors, are more rounded, lively, and lifelike. The lower half of the pot also shows much of the Geometric with bands of huddled water-birds, grazing fawns, and careless pattern work. The fawns, however, are less stiff than those of the Geometric period and the oblique zigzags are of Corinthian origin. The main zone on the upper belly of the pot shows two lions facing each other with a plant between and two long-necked birds picking at plants on each side below the handles of the pot. These are totally un-Geometric in their size and depiction.

A decade or two later, this same painter, on a neck amphora (Louvre Ca 2985; see Plate 1b) and on a bell krater (Munich 6077), shows little evidence of the Geometric tradition, except in some use of the silhouette, and even this is greatly modified by outline drawing of dress, reserved faces on most of his figures, free movement, and considerable use of incision. Though a bit crude, with carelessly drawn large figures of humans, animals and birds, the style is flowing and vital, far from the carefully controlled Geometric style (compare Plate 1b with Plate 1a).

By the second quarter of the seventh century B.C., the better painters had broken almost completely with the Geometric tradition. One of the great painters of the Black and White style has been called the *Painter of the Ram Jug* by Beazley.[5] This name was derived from his jug in Aegina depicting rams with the followers of Odysseus clinging under them in the escape from the cave of Polyphemos. Another earlier important work by this artist is the Aegisthus vase (Berlin A 32), an ovoid krater depicting Orestes, sword in hand, forcing Aegisthus forward to his death, with Clytemnestra preceeding and a fourth fragmentary figure following Orestes. Orestes is in black, but with an outline face and much incision for his hands, feet, dress, and ornaments. The other figures are in white with details drawn in black or brown lines.

The same painter's neck amphora in Berlin (Berlin A 9) is considered by Beazley[6] to be one of the masterpieces of Proto-Attic art. Depicted on the vase are, on one side, Pileus with the infant Achilles; on the other side is the centaur Chiron, an early example of simplicity in composition. The work of the Painter of the Ram Jug is illustrative of the fully developed Proto-Attic style of the 660s and 650s B.C. It is massive and monumental with drawing in both outline and silhouette, employing generous use of incision and white. His figures, though crude and ill-proportioned, appear to have rounded limbs and evidence life and force.

A stand in Berlin (Berlin A 42) has the name *Menelas*, inscribed beside one of five men pictured in the main scene. This is one of the earliest inscriptions known on a Greek vase. The decoration of this stand, in addition to Menelaos and his companions, includes three other friezes showing animals, sphinxes, and a cavalcade. The sphinxes and men are drawn partly in outline filled in with white without incision, while the animals are in black silhouette with much incision.

A neck amphora now in the Eleusis Museum (see Plate 1c) showing the blinding of the cyclops, Polyphemos, by Odysseus and two of his men is by the same painter as the Menelas stand.[7] Like others of its time, this vase combines reserved faces with incised black silhouette bodies for animals and men (except for Odysseus, from whom the original white coating has worn off). The gorgon sisters, Sthenno and Euryale, are done in a mixture of plain outline and of outline filled with white. This vase has little of the Geometric tradition other than certain features which were to be common to painted Greek pottery: sharp articulation, decoration in horizontal zones, and some use of silhouette.[8]

Another great Proto-Attic master is the *Painter of the New York Nessos Amphora*. His name-piece (New York 11.210.1; see Plate 1d) is large, comparing almost in size to the enormous Geometric neck amphorae, but evidencing a complete break from the Geometric in style of painting. On the neck are a lion and a spotted deer; on the shoulder are grazing horses; on the body of the pot, in a broad band, are shown Deianeira seated in a chariot with four horses, while Herakles chases the centaur Nettos. Numerous filling decorations are interspersed throughout the three scenes. The balance of the obverse and all of the reverse of the neck amphora are covered with various ornamental motifs. The figures are drawn partly in silhouette and partly in outline with strong rounded limbs. Dated between 670 and 650 B.C., this vase is fully representative of the Black and White style. Among the painter's other works is a fragmentary krater (Boston 6.67), which has recently been assigned to him.[9] Showing what appears to be the sacrifice of Iphigeneia, it is a more modest work, perhaps done later than the New York amphora, when the Black and White style was dying out.

LATE PROTO-ATTIC

In the years after the middle of the seventh century B.C., white was used less and purple began to appear as a major color. Briefly, there was a venture into polychrome painting, but the colors were not fast and this technique was abandoned. In general, vase painting became more disciplined. Planning became more thoughtful and less exuberant.

Notes on III — Origins of Attic Black-Figure

1. Chapter Three is based on Beazley, *Dev.*; Cook, *Greek P.P.*; Arias and Hirmer, *Greek Vase Painting;* and Martin Robertson, *Greek Painting* (Geneva: Skira, 1959).
2. Miss Richter (*Handbook,* p. 284) notes that some authorities refer to the period 720-650 B.C. as Idaean, and the period 650-600 as Daedalid, referring in each case to types of sculpture reflected in painted pottery.
3. See Cook, *Greek P.P.*, pp. 66-8.
4. Cook, *Greek P.P.*, p. 83, places the date around 705 B.C.; Beazley, *Dev.*, p. 5 and note 11, p. 105, lists this item as Athens N.M. 313 and dates it ca. 700 B.C.
5. Beazley, *Dev.*, pp. 8-12.
6. Ibid., p. 10.
7. The Berlin Menelas stand has been attributed to the Painter of the Ram Jug, and, according to Beazley, is at least close to his work. The painter also has been called the Menelas Painter and the Painter of the Berlin Menelas Stand. In addition, he has been called the Polyphemos Painter from the Eleusis vase.
8. Robertson, *Greek Painting,* p. 40.
9. Emily Vermeule and Suzanne Chapman, "A Protoattic Sacrifice?", *American Journal of Archaeology,* vol. 75, no. 3 (July 1971), pp. 285-93.

1a. Attic, Geometric neck-amphora. Ht. 160 cm. Funeral scene in handle zone; ca. 9th century B.C. Courtesy, National Archaeological Museum Athens. *See pp. 40 and 42.*

1b. Proto-Attic neck-amphora. Ht. 81 cm.; by the Analatos Painter. Upper zones: sphinxes; middle zone: dancers; belly zone: chariots; ca. 700-675 B.C. Courtesy, Musée du Louvre, Paris. *See p. 42.*

1c. Proto-Attic neck-amphora. Ht. 142 cm.; by the Menelas (or Polyphemos) Painter, Neck zone: blinding of Polyphemos; shoulder zone: animals; belly zone: Gorgons chasing Perseus; ca. 675-650 B.C. Courtesy, Eleusis Museum. *See p. 43.*

1d. Proto-Attic neck-amphora. Ht. 108.5 cm.; by the Painter of the New York Nessos Amphora (his name-piece). Neck zone: spotted deer and lion; shoulder zone: grazing horses; belly zone: Herakles, Nettos and Deianeira; ca. 675-650 B.C. Courtesy, The Metropolitan Museum of Art, Rogers Fund, 1911, New York.
See p. 43.

2a. Earliest Bf special neck-amphora. Ht. 122 cm.; by the Nettos Painter (his name-piece). Neck zone: Herakles killing Nettos; body zone: Medusa beheaded, her two gorgon sisters pursuing Perseus; ca. 615-600 B.C. Courtesy, National Archaeological Museum, Athens. See p. 110.

2b. Earliest Bf neck-amphora. Ht. 112 cm.; by the Piraeus Painter. Chariot scene; ca. 625-600 B.C. Courtesy, National Archaeological Museum, Athens. See p. 111.

2c. Early Bf neck-hydria, Corinthian type. Ht. 25.5 cm.; by the
Polos Painter. Corinthian designs: lions and sphinxes wearing
poloi; early sixth century B.C. Courtesy, Ecole Française
d'Archoelogie, Athens. See p. 112.

2d. Early Bf dinos with stand. Ht. with stand 93 cm.; Ht. of dinos alone 44 cm.; by the Gorgon Painter (his name-piece). Upper zone: Medusa beheaded, her two gorgon sisters pursuing Perseus; ca. 600-590 B.C. Courtesy, Musée du Louvre. See p. 112.

3a. Early Bf fragment of a dinos. Ht. of zone with horses 8 cm.; by Sophilos. Games for Patroklos above, lions below; ca. 580-570 B.C. Courtesy, National Archaeological Museum, Athens. See p. 113.

3b. *Early Bf Komast cup. Ht. 9.5 cm.; diam. of bowl 20.9 cm.; by the KX Painter. Komast dancers; ca. 590-570 B.C. Courtesy, The Metropolitan Museum of Art, Rogers Fund, 1922, New York. See p. 113.*

3c. *Early Bf skyphos. Ht. 10 cm.; by the KX Painter. Komast dancers; ca. 590-570 B.C. Courtesy, National Archaeological Museum, Athens. See p. 114.*

3d. Early Bf Siana cup (double-decker type). Ht. 13 cm.; diam. of bowl 24.5 cm.; by the C Painter. Achilles pursuing Troilos and Polyxena; ca. mid-sixth century B.C. Courtesy, The Metropolitan Museum of Art, Purchase 1901, New York. See p. 114.

4a. Early Bf neck-amphora, Tyrrhenian type. Ht. 38.7 cm.; by the Timiades Painter. Fight between warriors, sphinx between panthers, goat between panthers; ca. 575-550 B.C. Courtesy, The Metropolitian Museum of Art, Collection of Dean K. Boorman and published with his kind permission. See p. 115.

4b. Early Bf amphora, Type B, Panel type. Ht. 38.3 cm.; unattributed. Horse's Head; ca. 560-550 B.C. Courtesy, The Metropolitan Museum of Art, Fletcher Fund, 1926, New York. See p. 16.

4c. Early Bf oval lekythos. Ht. 17.5 cm.; by the Pharos Painter. Two women wrapped in one large cloak; ca. 575-550 B.C. Courtesy, The Metropolitan Museum of Art, Gift of Samuel G. Ward, 1875, New York. See p. 31.

4d. Early Bf early shoulder lekythos. Ht. 18.7 cm.; unattributed. Panther and deer; ca. mid-sixth century B.C. Courtesy, The Metropolitan Museum of Art, the Theodore M. Davis Collection; Bequest of Theodore M. Davis, 1915, New York. See p. 31.

*5a. Mature Bf volute-krater, "The François Vase." Ht. 66 cm.;
by Kleitias. Narrative style in bands showing legends and
animals; ca. 570 B.C. Courtesy, Museo Archeologico, Firenze.
See p. 121.*

5b. Mature Bf dinos. Ht. 49 cm.; by the Painter of Acropolis 606 (his name-piece). Battle scenes; ca. 575-550 B.C. Courtesy, National Archaeological Museum, Athens. See p. 121.

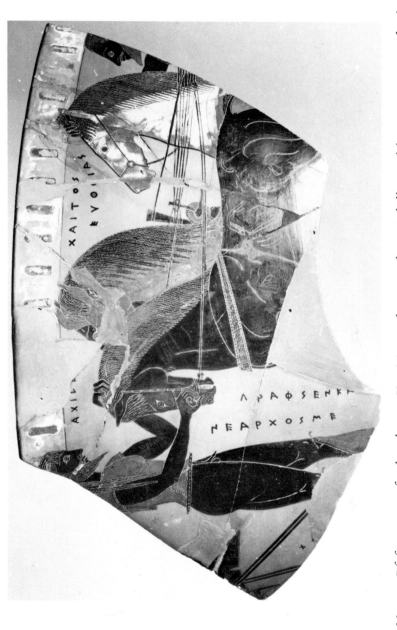

5c. Mature Bf fragment of a kantharas. Ht. 15 cm.; by Nearchos. Achilles and horses preparing for battle; ca. 575-550 B.C. Courtesy, National Archaeological Museum, Athens. See p. 122.

5d. Mature Bf column-krater. Ht. 55.9 cm.; by Lydos. Hephaestos returning to Olympos escorted by Dionysos, satyrs and maenads; ca. 550-540 B.C. Courtesy, The Metropolitan Museum of Art, Fletcher Fund, 1931, New York. *See p. 122.*

*6a. Mature Bf amphora, type B. Ht. 39 cm.; by the Amasis
Painter. Warriors arming; ca. 550-540 B.C. Courtesy, The Met-
ropolitan Museum of Art, Rogers Fund, 1906, New York.
See p. 123.*

6b. Mature Bf amphora, Type C. Ht. 41.4 cm.; by the Affecter.
Dionysos and his followers; ca. 550-530 B.C. Courtesy, The Met-
ropolitan Museum of Art, Rogers Fund, 1918, New York.
See p. 123.

6c. Mature Bf neck-hydria. Ht. 32.5 cm.; by Elbows Out. Return of Hephaestos; mid-sixth century B.C. Courtesy, Museum of Fine Arts, Boston, Catherine Page Perkins Collection. See p. 124.

6d. Mature Bf amphora, Type B. Ht. 40.1 cm.; by the Swing Painter (his name-piece). Girl in a swing and four men; mid-sixth century B.C. Courtesy, Museum of Fine Arts, Boston. H.L. Pierce Fund. See p. 124.

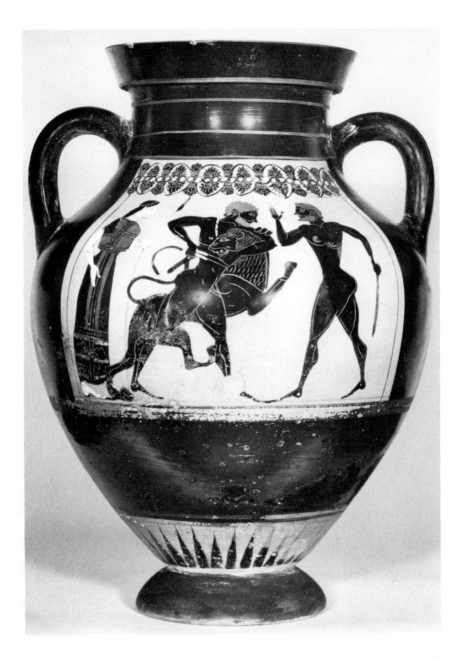

7a. Mature Bf amphora, Type B. Ht. as restored 37.8 cm.; by
Group E. Herakles and the Nemean Lion; ca. 540 B.C.
Courtesy, The Metropolitan Museum of Art, Fletcher Fund,
1956, New York. See p. 124.

7b. Mature Bf neck-amphora, Type A, with lid. Ht. 47 cm.; by Exekias. Marriage procession, perhaps of Herakles and Hebe; ca. 540 B.C. Courtesy, The Metropolitan Museum of Art, Rogers Fund, 1917, New York. See p. 124.

7c. *Mature Bf amphora, Type A. Ht. 61 cm.; by Exekias. Achilles and Ajax playing at dice during a lull in battle; ca. 540-530 B.C. Courtesy of the Museum Etrusco Gregoriano, Vatican. See pp. 124 and 125.*

*7d. Mature Bf neck-amphora, Type A. Ht. 41.3 cm.; by Exekias.
Achilles killing the Amazon queen Penthesilea; ca. 530 B.C.
By courtesy of the Trustees of the British Museum, London.
See pp. 124 and 125.*

8a. Mature Bf lip-cup (alien foot). Ht. 19.6 cm.; diam. of bowl 28.5 cm.; by the Phrynos Painter and signed by the potter Phrynos. Birth of Athena; mid-sixth century B.C. By courtesy of the Trustees of the British Museum, London. See p. 126.

8b. *Mature Bf lip-cup. Ht. 17.5 cm., diam. 21.7 cm.; attributed to the Tleson Painter. The signature of the potter Tleson and palmettes are the only decoration; ca. 550-525 B.C. Courtesy, The Metropolitan Museum of Art. Purchase, 1955, Christos G. Bastis Gift, New York. See p. 126.*

8c. *Mature Bf band-cup. Ht. 16.4 cm., diam. 28.4 cm.; unattributed. Dionysos and Ariadne with satyrs and maenads; ca. 550-520 B.C. Courtesy, The Metropolitan Museum of Art, Rogers Fund, 1917, New York. See p. 28.*

8d. *Mature Bf Cassel cup. Ht. 8.7 cm., diam. of bowl 13.4 cm.; unattributed; ca. 550-525 B.C. Courtesy, The Metropolitan Museum of Art, New York. See p. 29.*

9a. Mature Bf Droop cup. Ht. 12.8 cm., diam. of bowl 25.4 cm.; by the Group of Rhodes 12264. Battle of Greeks and Amazons; ca. 550-525 B.C. Courtesy, The Metropolitan Museum of Art, Rogers Fund, 1906, New York. See p. 29.

9b. *Mature Bf Proto-A cup. Ht. 11.4 cm., diam. of bowl 20.3 cm.; by the Painter of Louvre F28. Birth of Athena from the forehead of Zeus, meaningless inscriptions; ca. mid-sixth century B.C. Courtesy, The Metropolitan Museum of Art, Rogers Fund, 1906, New York.*

9c. Mature Bf eye-cup (or Type A). Ht. 11.9 cm., diam. of bowl 30.5 cm.; unattributed. Head of Dionysos between "apotropaic eyes"; ca. 525 B.C. Courtesy, Museum of Art, Rhode Island School of Design, Providence. See p. 30.

9d. *Late Bf one-piece cup (or Type B). Ht. 6.5 cm., diam. of bowl 14.9 cm.; in the manner of the Haimon Painter. Satyrs and maenads; ca. 500-475 B.C. Courtesy, The Metropolitan Museum of Art, Rogers Fund, 1941, New York. See p. 31.*

10a. *Late Bf stemless kylix. Ht. 7.0 cm., diam. of bowl 18.2 cm.; unattributed. Lions, ca. 530-500 B.C. Published by permission of The M. H. De Young Memorial Museum, San Francisco.*

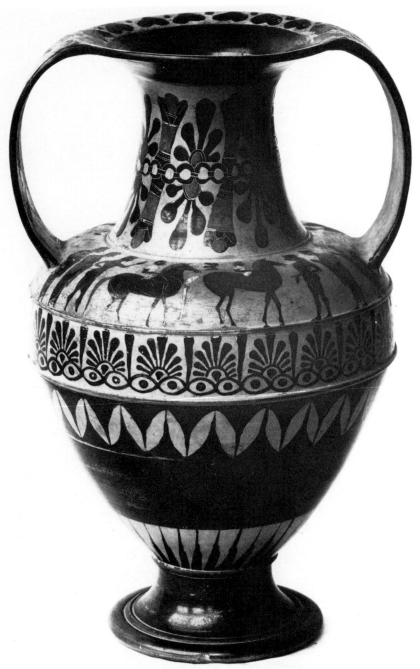

10b. Bf neck-amphora, Nikosthenic type. Ht. 28.6 cm.; unattributed, but signed by the potter Nikosthenes. Two horsemen between six figures; late sixth century B.C. Courtesy, Museum of Art, Rhode Island School of Design, Providence. See pp. 21 and 22.

10c. Late Bf amphora, Type A. Ht. 53.2 cm.; by the Lysippides Painter. Apotheosis of Herakles with Athena, Dionysos, Kore and Hermes; ca. 530-520 B.C. Courtesy, The Metropolitan Museum of Art. Gift of Col. and Mrs. Lewis Landes, 1958, New York. See p. 131.

10d. Late Bf neck-hydria. Ht. 51.1 cm.; by the Antimenes Painter. Harnessing of Athena's chariot; ca. 520-500 B.C. Courtesy, The Minneapolis Institute of Art, The John R. Van Derlip Fund, Minneapolis. See p. 132.

11a. Late Bf neck-hydria. Ht. 54.1 cm.; by the Leagros Group. Ajax and Achilles playing at dice; ca. 515-510 B.C. Courtesy, The Metropolitan Museum of Art, Fletcher Fund, 1956, New York. See p. 132.

11b. Late Bf amphora, Type A. Ht. 51.1 cm.; by the Rycroft Painter.
Chariot drawn by four horses abreast; ca. 525 B.C. Courtesy, The
Metropolitan Museum of Art, Rogers Fund, 1906, New York.
See p. 133.

11c. Mature Bf amphora, Type B. Ht. 39.2 cm.; by the BMN Painter. Theseus killing the Minotaur; ca. 540 B.C. Courtesy, Museum of Fine Arts, Boston, Otis Norcross Fund. See p. 133.

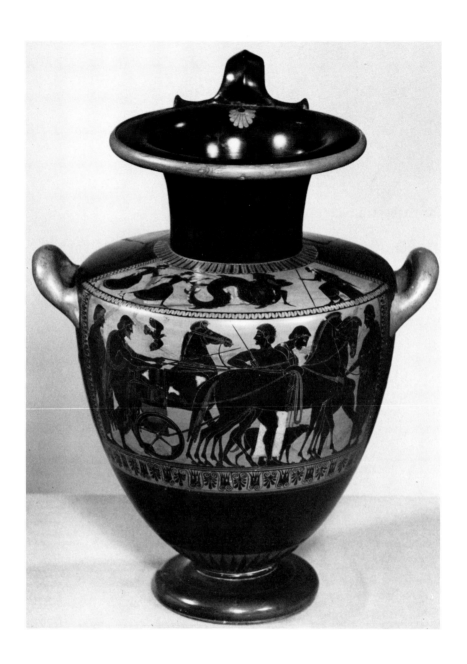

11d. Late Bf neck-hydria. Ht. with handle 47 cm.; by Psiax.
Harnessing of chariot; ca. 530-500 B.C. Courtesy, Wadsworth
Atheneum, Ella Gallup Sumner and Mary Catlin Sumner Col-
lection, Hartford. See p. 134.

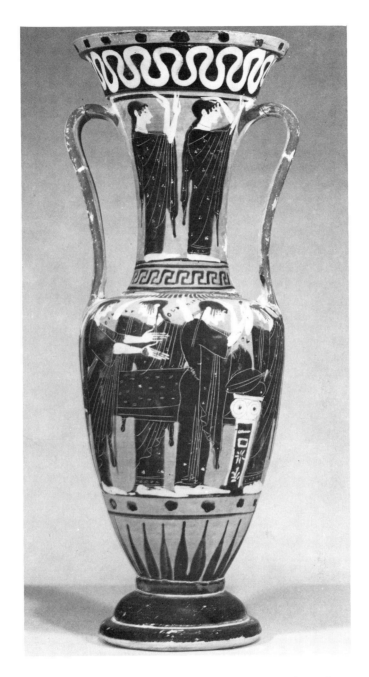

12a. Late Bf loutrophoros. Ht. 43.5 cm.; unattributed. Mourning women; late sixth century B.C. Courtesy, The Cleveland Museum of Art. Purchase, Charles W. Harkness Fund, Cleveland. See p. 34.

12b. Late Bf oinochoe. Ht. 23 cm.; unattributed, painted on white background. Scene of combat, ca. 500-475 B.C. Courtesy, The Fogg Art Museum, Harvard University, Cambridge. See p. 35.

12c. *Late Bf lekythos. Ht. 27.7 cm.; by the Gela Painter, painted on white background. Herakles and Pholos; ca. 500 B.C. Courtesy, Museum of Fine Arts, Gift of E.P. Warren, Boston. See p. 135.*

12d. Late Bf neck-amphora, small special type. Ht. 26.7 cm.; by the Edinburgh Painter. Athletes; early fifth century B.C. Courtesy, The Metropolitan Museum of Art, Gift of El Conde de Lagunillos, 1956, New York. See p. 136.

13a. Late Bf lekythos. Ht. 14.8 cm.; by the Marathon Painter, painted on white background. Women dancing before an image of Dionysos; ca. 490 B.C. Courtesy, The Metropolitan Museum of Art, Gift of Samuel G. Ward, 1875, New York. See p. 136.

13b. Late Bf lekythos. Ht. 17.9 cm.; by the Sappho Painter, painted on white background. Helios, Nyx and Eros; ca. 500-490 B.C. Courtesy, The Metropolitan Museum of Art, Rogers Fund, 1941, New York. *See p. 136.*

13c. Late Bf lekythos. Ht. 25.4 cm.; by the Diosphos Painter, painted on white background. Death of Medusa; ca. 485-460 B.C. Courtesy, The Metropolitan Museum of Art, Rogers Fund, 1906, New York. See p. 137.

13d. Late Bf skyphos. Ht. 16.2 cm., diam. of bowl 22.4 cm.; by the Theseus Painter. Poseidon on a sea-horse; ca. 500 B.C. Courtesy, The Metropolitan Museum of Art, Rogers Fund, 1917, New York. See p. 137.

14a. Late Bf lekythos. Ht. 34.6 cm.; by the Athena Painter, painted on white background. Battle of Gods and Giants; ca. 480 B.C. Courtesy, The Metropolitan Museum of Art, Rogers Fund 1907, New York. *See p. 137.*

14b. Late Bf lekythos. Ht. 34.6 cm.; by the Haimon Painter, painted on white background. Procession of lyrists and castanet players; ca. early fifth century B.C. Courtesy, The Metropolitan Museum of Art, Rogers Fund, 1941, New York. See p. 137.

14c. Late Bf "chimney" lekythos. Ht. 27.8 cm.; by the Emporion Painter, painted on both orange-red and white background. Female and Triton; ca. 470 B.C. Courtesy, The Metropolitan Museum of Art, Rogers Fund, 1941, New York. See p. 138.

14d. Early Bf Panathenaic amphora, "The Burgon Vase." Ht.
61 cm.; by the Burgon Group; ca. 570-560 B.C. By courtesy of
the Trustees of the British Museum, London. See p. 23.

15a. Late Bf Panathenaic amphora. Ht. 62.2 cm.; by the Euphiletos Painter; ca. 520 B.C. Courtesy, The Metropolitan Museum, Rogers Fund, 1914, New York. See p. 23.

15b. Late Bf Panathenaic amphora. Ht. 64.8 cm.; by the Leagros Group; ca. 510 B.C. Courtesy, The Metropolitan Museum of Art, Rogers Fund, 1907, New York. See pp. 23 and 132.

15c. Late Bf Panathenaic amphora. Ht. 64.8 cm.; by the Kleoph-rades Painter; ca. 500 B.C. Courtesy, The Metropolitan Museum of Art, Rogers Fund, 1907, New York. See p. 23.

*15d. Bf Panathenaic amphora. Ht. 73.9 cm.; by the Kuban Group;
end of the fifth century B.C. By courtesy of the Trustees of the
British Museum, London. See p. 24.*

16a. Bf Panathenaic amphora. Ht. 71.2 cm.; by the Polyzelos Group; ca. 366 B.C. By courtesy of the Trustees of the British Museum, London. See p. 24.

16b. Bf Panathenaic amphora. Ht. 81.3 cm.; unattributed; ca. 340-339 B.C. Courtesy, The Fogg Art Museum, Harvard University, Cambridge. See p. 24.

16c. Bf Panathenaic amphora. Ht. 82.7 cm.; by the Hobble Group;
ca. 336 B.C. By courtesy of the Trustees of the British Museum,
London. See p. 24.

16d. Bf Panathenaic amphora. Ht. with lid, 79 cm.; unattributed; Hellenistic, second century B.C. Courtesy, Staatliche Museen Preussischer Kulturbesitz, Antikenabteilung, VI 4950, Berlin. See p. 25.

Early Development of Attic Black-Figure[1]

TRANSITION FROM PROTO-ATTIC TO ATTIC BLACK-FIGURE

The Attic black-figure technique evolved during the last quarter of the seventh century B.C., as a result of the coincidence of several factors. Incision, reds, and white had been borrowed earlier in that century from Corinth and had been incorporated into the Proto-Attic style. Late in the seventh century, Athenian vase painters began to adopt the Corinthian Animal style of painting. This involved depiction of black silhouette animals and fantastic creatures together with the use of filling ornaments within the main picture. About the same time, Athenian potters began to utilize the firing properties of Attic clay to produce an orange-red for the background and an improved black for the silhouette.[2] Thus, gradually, were brought together all the essential elements of what is defined as the Attic black-figure technique.[3]

Various explanations have been offered for readoption of the silhouette in the second quarter of the seventh century after its abandonment for many years.[4] It has been suggested that balance of light and dark had been of concern to Greek vase painters since the Protogeometric period and that the black silhouette offered a return to this balance. Another possible reason for returning to the silhouette is that it does not tend to thin and distort on the curved surface of the pot, whereas outline figures do. In addition, outline drawing against a light background tends to appear meager. Finally, the exuberance and chaos of the Proto-Attic style had run counter to the Greek love of order, and the silhouette provided order.

The transition from the Proto-Attic style to Attic black-figure was, of course, gradual. Outline drawing persisted; thus, silhouette figures appeared alongside outline figures, or bodies were drawn in silhouette, but given outline faces. Massiveness of composition and looseness of drawing continued for a time to characterize the main pictures, while subsidiary friezes were more carefully controlled. Shapes remained relatively large, as they had been in the Proto-Attic period.[5]

The hazy division between late Proto-Attic and earliest black-figure may be seen in the overlapping of dates, 650-610 B.C. for the former and 625-600 B.C. for the latter; it is also evident in the work of various painters who span this uncertain boundary with some of their early work still Proto-Attic, but with their later work clearly black-figure.

EARLIEST BLACK-FIGURE ca. 625-600 B.C.

Earliest black-figure painting was a blend of Proto-Attic, Corinthian influence, and new colors developed in the Athenian workshops.

The earliest black-figure painters drew large compositions on relatively large pots in the Proto-Attic tradition.

From Corinth, they drew their themes and ornamentation. Thus, sphinxes, chimerae, sirens, gorgons, and lions dominated the main panels, though processions of women, chariots, and scenes from mythology also were shown. Filling ornaments (rosettes, stalked rosettes, spirals, and sigmas) were scattered around the main picture, while the frame usually had spiral hooks and hooked triangles intruding into the panels. Subsidiary panels depicted fierce animals in pairs or locked in combat as well as fawns and goats. Among birds were cocks, owls, and geese. Floral designs included base rays and, sometimes, palmette and lotus designs.

The silhouettes were painted in the new improved black against the new orange-red background.

Beazley lists five painters as belonging in the earliest black-figure period.[6] Among these, by far the most important is the *Nettos (or Nessos) Painter,* whose work bridges the uncertain zone between the Proto-Attic and true black-figure techniques. His name-piece is a large neck-amphora (Athens 1002; see Plate 2a) portraying Herakles and the centaur Nettos (name inscribed on the vase). This work is still largely Proto-Attic with its massive figures, filling ornaments and hooked triangles. His later work, however, is fully black-figure in its derivation from Corinthian models, its free use of silhouette, incision and purple, employment of panels and narrow bands, and sparing use of white. Especially is Corinthian influence evident in his gorgon heads, intricate floral patterns, and discreet use of filling ornaments. His monumental figures are drawn with generous, sure, sweeping lines, have large features, serious expressions, and appear solidly rounded. In his later work, he often depicts friezes of ferocious monsters and lively animals. Twenty-eight items are attributed to him and an additional seventeen are near his work or are at least comparable.[7] The work of the Nettos Painter may be dated approximately from 615 to 605 B.C.

Another important painter of this period is the *Piraeus Painter*, who may have preceded the Nettos Painter. Though his work clearly is influenced by the Corinthian style of painting, his animals are powerful, ponderous, and massive. He depicted chariots, loop work, cocks, and floral designs with neat filling ornamentation on his two attributed works (see Plate 2b).

EARLY BLACK-FIGURE ca. 610-550 B.C.

Painters whose works are included under the heading "early black-figure" are those who abandoned the Proto-Attic tradition and adopted the Corinthian influence.

At first, both Corinthian shapes and its Animal style with monsters, normal animals, birds, usual florae, and subsidiary designs were embraced almost completely. In contrast to the "earliest black-figure" painters, who had drawn large compositions on relatively large pots, "early black figure" painters drew small compositions on small pots. They crowded their animals into bands and friezes, often grouping them in threes, fours or fives — for example, a siren or pair of sirens between two lions, with other animals outside facing the center. Initially, the animals were more individualized and more lively than the Corinthian. By 590 B.C., however, they had become lifeless[8] or simply stereotyped copies of the Corinthian models.[9]

There were, of course, some human figures shown on vases from the beginning of Attic black-figure. At first, however, they were drawn from Corinthian models, including mourning women, chariot scenes, the battle of Lapiths and centaurs, fights among warriors, and the return of Hephaestos.

The second and third decades of the early black-figure period seem to have been characterized by mass-production, probably reflecting Attic attempts to flood markets previously dominated by Corinth.[10] Use of white and red with much incision was characteristic in this period. Quality of painting was generally poor.

Among the more interesting items classified as early black-figure are the Komast cups, the Siana cups and Tyrrhenian amphorae.

About fifty painters and groups[11] are classified as falling within the "early black-figure" category.

Pot Painters

Most of the artists of the early black-figure period painted on pots[12], many on smaller items including lekythoi, various types of lekanides, and plates, though the better artists decorated larger pots such as various types of amphorae, kraters, and dinoi.

Among the painters of pots, the *Polos Painter* deserves mention if only because he was so prolific (192 items are attributed to him) and because he is representative of an early trend towards uncritical acceptance of Corinthian shapes and Animal style in the years 590 — 570 B.C. (see Plate 2c). His name, incidentally, comes from the pill-box hats (or *poloi*) worn by his women, sirens, and sphinxes.

Far more important is the *Gorgon Painter,* the chief representative of a new generation of painters. Named after his picture of a gorgon on a dinos in Paris (Louvre E 847; see Plate 2d), he is credited with a total of forty-one items and there are another sixty-one in his manner. Though his animal friezes and floral complexes clearly evidence the effect of the Corinthian influence, he imparts to his animals a degree of individual character rarely found in Corinthian painting. Indeed, he appears to be the last of the Attic artists truly interested in animals, though others continued their use for many years, especially in subsidiary friezes. He arranged his animals in groups of from three to five, often with one or a pair between two facing animals. Though he tended to fill all areas of his vases with zones of animal or other decorations, the fields of these zones usually are relatively clear of filling ornament. His style is characterized by use of expressive gestures, careful drawing, and clear, simple, symmetrical compositions. His figures, however, are tame and limp in comparison with those of the Nettos Painter.

The names *Sophilos* inscribed on two dinoi (Athens Acr. 587 and Athens 15 499) are the earliest known examples of signatures by an Attic painter.[13] Sophilos also signed as potter on three items (Athens 15 499 — mentioned above — Athens 2035.1, and a dinos in London in the collection of the Hon. Robert Erskine). Once called the "Marathon Painter," he is not to be confused with the later painter of lekythoi, now given that name.

Some authorities have suggested that the Gorgon Painter is an earlier phase of Sophilos and that the KX Painter may also be Sophilos in another phase.[14] Neither suggestion appears to be accepted by archaeologists today. It appears that both Sophilos and the KX Painter were followers of the Gorgon Painter, or that Sophilos and the Gorgon Painter were from the same school. Though ambitious, Sophilos is regarded as a lesser artist than the Gorgon Painter.

Some forty-seven works are attributed to Sophilos with fourteen others possibly by him or at least near his style. Not a very good draftsman, his style is clumsier and more labored than that of the Gorgon Painter. He used Corinthian shapes and though he painted animal friezes, he loosened the Corinthian influence by his acute observation of nature. He was best at drawing large massive figures; when he drew small figures, his hand was much less sure. He tended to make lavish use of white for the flesh of women and horses (directly over the clay with no undercoating) and is the only Attic artist of the period to use matte red and purple for the outline and inner lines of figures. He was painstaking in his detail of humans and their dress. Like others of his time, he painted animals in rows as well as mythological characters including Artemis, Hermes, Menelaos, and Helen, Herakles, mourning women (on his plaques), and satyrs. His satyrs, incidentally, are among the earliest depicted and he is the first to attempt to show a building. One of his most famous pieces is a dinos fragment depicting the games at the funeral of Patroklos (see Plate 3a). His work dates to the period 590-570 B.C.

Cup Painters

Komast Cups ca. 585-570 B.C.

Cups and skyphoi of the Komast Group are shapes borrowed from Corinth and are painted in a style evidencing strong influence from that city. No painter's signatures have been found on any of these cups; accordingly, names have been assigned to five artists who can be distinguished. Two of these are discussed below.

The *KX Painter*[15] is probably the founder of the Komast Group, though he is credited with only three Komast cups and nine skyphoi showing the *komos*, or "dancing reveler" (see Plates 3b and

3c). An excellent painter, his recognized works include forty-three items. An additional fifteen may be by him; at least, they are in his manner. In addition to his komos scenes and his somewhat infrequent scenes from mythology (at which he was best), he depicted animals in rows, men and women, and chariots. His work dates from the period 590-570 B.C.

The *KY Painter* is another major painter of the Komast Group. Though more prolific than the KX Painter in depicting komos scenes (twenty-two Komast cups and three skyphoi are recognized as his work), he is not quite so good a painter. In all, he has thirty-two assigned works with eight others probably by him or at least in his manner. In addition to the komos scene, he depicted the usual Corinthian repertoire of animals and birds on his larger items. His work falls into the first quarter of the sixth century.

Siana Cups ca. 575-550 B.C.

About one decade after the appearance of the Komast cups, Attic potters developed a new cup shape now known as the Siana cup. This shape, though completely Attic, continued to be painted under Corinthian influence. The better cups of this type have been attributed to some fifteen painters and groups. Among these is the master painter, Lydos (who is discussed later in another context). Two specialists in Siana cups produced between them the vast majority of the attributed cups of this type.

The *C (for Corinthianizing) Painter* was the most prolific among painters of Siana cups. Of his 162 clearly attributed works, 110 are of the "overlap" Siana type and twenty-five are "double-deckers," while six others include merrythought, near-lip and Proto A cups (see Plate 3d). In addition, some twenty to thirty-five other items are in his manner or related. He owes much to the Corinthian influence for his favorite subjects and lavish use of incision, white and purple, yet he is fully Attic in the free use of fine orange-red clay and shiny black. He placed his white over a black or brown undercoat. Strangely, while he made much use of incision, he did not employ it in drawing the cornea of the eye. His colors are cheerful. His figures are short, thick-set, and often quaint, but clear and lively. Generally, he confined his pictures to the main elements, though he evidenced a gift for vivid narrative on some of his works. A specialist in cups, some of his best work is, however, on other shapes. His favorite scenes include athletic events, cavalcades of warriors or youths, and battle scenes. Typical of his work are incised shield devices.

The other major painter of Siana cups was the *Heidelberg Painter,* who has some sixty-nine attributed works and eight items which are very close or recall his style. His name comes from a cup in the Heidelberg museum (Heidelberg VI 29 a). Of his attributed works, thirty-nine are "overlap" and seventeen are "double-decker" Siana cups, while ten others are too fragmentary to differentiate. Apparently a colleague of the C Painter, he also is very close to the Amasis Painter. His favorite scenes include gods and goddesses, Herakles, satyrs, maenads, dancers, men and youths, and scenes from Troy. He often put swans beneath the handles of his cups. Characteristic of his work are spectators watching the main event.

Painters of Tyrrhenian Amphorae ca. 575-550 B.C.

A special type of neck-amphora was developed in the Attic workshops about the same time as the Siana cups. The decoration of these new neck-amphora, like that of the cups, shows a strong Corinthian influence with depictions of sphinxes, heraldic animals, lions, and panthers. Both in shape and in decoration, they were probably made to attract the Etruscan market. About 175 of these ovoid neck-amphorae have been found to date. Some 120 of these vases have been assigned to eight painters and three groups.[16] As none of the artists signed their works, they have been given names by archaeologists. Three of the more prominent are mentioned below.

The *Castellani Painter* was the most prolific, with thirty-seven attributed items. Named after one of his vases once in the Castellani collection (now at Villa Giulia), his works often have dicing separating the shoulder friezes from the animal bands below. His favorite shield device seems to have been a panther protome.[17]

The *Timiades Painter,* whose name is derived from the name of the fallen warrior depicted on one of his vases (Boston 98.916), is rather unique. Unlike most of the painters of Tyrrhenian amphorae, his inscriptions make sense. His mythology also is interesting. He depicted cocks, boars, and panthers often in heraldic arrangement, but never goats or bulls (see Plate 4a). He is credited with at least twenty-four of these ovoid neck-amphorae.

The *Goltyr Painter,*[18] to whom eighteen of these special amphorae are attributed, often included boar hunts, komoi, centauromachies, amazonomachies and Herakles above with rows of animals below.

TRANSITION FROM EARLY TO MATURE BLACK-FIGURE ca. 570-550 B.C.

The years 570 to 550 B.C. witnessed a gradual abandonment of the Corinthian influence and the development of new shapes and a truly Attic style of painting. Some potters and painters, perhaps the older ones, clung to the former styles and hence are considered to be still "early black-figure" artists. Others, probably younger men, who developed new shapes, new styles, and new concepts of composition and abandoned the old conventions, may be considered as "mature black-figure" painters. Early and mature black-figure thus coexisted for about two decades.

The Animal style of painting, borrowed from Corinth, which had dominated early black-figure work and which had become lifeless or stereotyped, received a brief injection of new life and elegance from the miniaturists of the second quarter of the sixth century.[19] By 550 B.C., however, the Animal style was dying out, being replaced by an Attic Human style. Thereafter, though the tradition of animal figures continued, animals were relegated to subordinate friezes. As such, they continued to appear on black-figured vases until the end of the sixth century.

The two decades after about 570 B.C. were years in which various concepts of composition evolved, as painters turned from the small crowded animal friezes of the earlier period. Some painters painted monumental scenes. Other sought elegance in miniatures. Still others painted in narrative style, showing battles and other events from mythology in bands running around their pots. The general trend, however, was towards a single large composition made up of a compact group of a few human figures framed within bands of subsidiary decoration.

During these same years, certain old conventions were replaced by new. Filling ornamentation was gradually eliminated. By 570 B.C., it had become conventional to depict the flesh of men black (prior to 570 B.C. with purple faces)[20] and the flesh of women white (generally over a black base). Soon after, it became conventional to paint the female eye as an elongated almond in contrast to the rounded male eye.[21] By mid-sixth century B.C., outline drawing had reappeared for occasional use.[22] Portrayal of the human figure also began to evolve around 550 B.C. Throughout the era of the black-figure technique the human body was normally portrayed as having a profile head and legs and a frontal torso. About 550 B.C., however, tentative attempts were made to show the body not as just a frontal and profile combination. By mid-sixth century drapery, which previously had been stiff and flat, finally was somewhat softened and shown with folds.

By 550 B.C., though traces of Corinthian influence and of the Animal style remained, black-figure had become a truly Attic style and Corinth had been eliminated both as a major influence on style and as a competitor in the market. Athens became the ceramic center of the Mediterranean world.[23]

Notes on IV — Early Development of Attic Black-Figure

1. Throughout Chapters Four through Six I have drawn heavily on Beazley's *ABV, Sketch, Dev.,* and *Paralipomena,* as well as Cook's *Greek P.P.*, Arias and Hirmer's *Greek Vase Painting,* and Robertson's *Greek Painting.*

2. Corinthian clay fired greenish-white, sometimes with a pinkish tinge, so that Corinthian black-figured works showed a black silhouette against a whitish background. Proto-Attic figures also had been painted against a whitish background with a black which frequently fired poorly to a reddish hue.

3. See Chapter One, Section entitled "Essential Elements."

4. Beazley, *Sketch,* p. 9.

5. As noted earlier, in Chapter Two, borrowing of smaller shapes from Corinth occurred a little later, early in the sixth century.

6. Beazley, *ABV,* Chapter I.

7. Including works formerly attributed to the "Chimaera Painter." Attributions are by Beazley in *ABV,* as amended by *Paralipomena,* unless otherwise stated. Such phrases as "comparable," "related," "near his style," "in his manner," etc. refer to works close in style to a painter, but not yet attributed to him. See Appendix I.

8. Typical of the animals of Sophilos and his followers.

9. The Polos Painter and his group uncritically accepted the Corinthian styles and shapes; see Cook, *Greek P.P.,* p. 77.

10. Robertson, *Greek Painting,* p. 57.

11. The term "group" refers to a series of items closely related in style of painting, but which, as yet, have not been assigned to a particular painter.

12. As distinguished from various cup forms.

13. Timonidas of Corinth signed as painter about the same time.

14. See below for the KX Painter.

15. The KX Painter and the following KY Painter have been given these names by archaeologists to designate Painters Y and X of the group of painters of Komast cups.

16. Painters of Tyrrhenian amphorae are also credited with decorating some twenty other shapes.

17. von Bothmer, "Painters of Tyrrhenian Vases."

18. Goltyr is a contraction of Goluchow and Tyrrhenian, in recognition of one of his amphorae, Goluchow 7.

19. Cook, *Greek P.P.,* p. 77. The animals of Kleitias and the Little Masters are examples.

20. Ibid., p. 72.

21. There were, of course, exceptions in which the female eyes were drawn the same as the male eyes.

22. Outline drawing was rare throughout the years of the black-figure technique, but it never died out entirely, being used from time to time in drawing the faces and arms of women and for horses (e.g., Sophilos, Nearchos, and the Amasis Painter).

23. Richter, *Handbook,* p. 305.

V

The Masters of Attic Black-Figure

MATURE BLACK-FIGURE ca. 570-525 B.C.

When finally freed of Corinthian influence, Attic vase painting is classified as "mature black-figure." Almost one hundred painters and groups have been placed in this category. In the following pages, we will trace the development of the black-figure technique to its apogee. The main lines are followed in the works of six master painters: Kleitias, the Painter of Acropolis 606, Nearchos Lydos, the Amasis Painter and Exekias. Along with these are mentioned other prominent painters of the period. A few of these were outside the mainstreams of evolution. The Affecter and Elbows Out, for example, though excellent technicians, were consciously old-fashioned "mannerists." The Swing Painter, the Painter of Louvre F6, and the painters of Group E are mentioned both for their abilities and because of the large number of works attributed to them.

The narrative style was of brief duration in mature black-figure. Its peak was reached very early in the "François Vase" painted by Kleitias about the year 570 B.C. The style of painting on this vase is thoroughly Attic. The drawing is meticulous in detail and in use of titles to identify the characters shown. Though the narrative style was employed for some years longer, no succeeding artists are known who surpassed the narrative style of Kleitias.

The current of miniaturist painting continued throughout the period of mature black-figure painting, especially on lip, band, and

119

other Little Master cups as well as on eye-cups, which appeared late in the mature period. Painting on these items often was elegant with fine incision. Among their decorators are found many excellent painters such as the Phrynos Painter and the Tleson Painter as well as some of the great masters of the black-figure technique.

The major current, however, was towards portrayal of a single scene on larger vessels. The Painter of Acropolis 606 and Nearchos are among the greater artists using this type of composition in the years 570-550 B.C. In the following quarter century, newer and greater artists depicted masterful scenes from mythology. Equilibrium of composition was characteristic of the better works, on which were shown one or at most a few important characters. Portrayal of mood replaced narrative rendition.

Thus, scenes from the Iliad were heroic, dignified, sombre, often grim or pathetic, while illustrations of the Dionysiac cycle of myths were ribald, gay, and amusing. These works serve as beautiful illustrations from the ancient myths and legends. Lydos and the Amasis Painter are among the great painters in this type of composition; the former often produced works of grandeur; the latter was at his best in gay, slightly irreverent Dionysiac scenes. Exekias, more grave in outlook, was the master at capturing a single highly significant moment, often the moment of crisis. With the work of these men Attic black-figure reached its peak.

During the mature black-figure period Athenian potters continued to improve upon the old Type B amphora and developed the Type A amphora. The former became the favorite shape of the better painters of the period with the latter in second place. Meanwhile, many potters had turned to the production of new cup shapes. Among these, lip-cups and band-cups became the favorites of the Little Master miniaturists. Near the end of the mature period the special Nikosthenic neck-amphora and the eye-cup (or Type A cup) were developed.

Pot Painters

The best artists of the mature phase of Attic black-figure painted on large pots, though some of them also decorated small vessels and cups as a sideline. In this section, we will glance first at the work of the chief exponent of the narrative style and then trace the development of the single large composition to its peak and the beginning of its decline.

Kleitias is the greatest master of the early years of the mature black-figure period. Though credited with sixteen items (and with an additional eight near his style), he is best known for his famous volute krater, the "François Vase" (Florence 4209; see Plate 5a). This krater bears Kleitias' signature as painter and that of Ergotimos as potter. It was found in many fragments scattered over a wide area just outside the Etruscan city of Chiusi by an Italian excavator, Allessandro François, whose name it bears. The François Vase is the epitome of the narrative style. Decorated with six bands running around the neck and body of the pot and with one band on the base it tells several stories.[1] On one side of the lip, Theseus returns from Crete, on the other side is the Calydonian boar-hunt. On one side of the neck is the battle of Centaurs and Lapiths, on the other the funeral games for Patroklos. The main frieze on the body shows the wedding procession at the marriage of Peleus and Thetis encircling the entire pot. Below this on one side is depicted the return of Hephaestos and on the other the ambushing of Troilos. Next below is a frieze of animals and, lastly, a band of rays. On the foot, is the battle between the pygmies and the cranes. On the handles are other figures. In all, there are more than two hundred, many of them identified by inscriptions, and all beautifully done.

Kleitias signed four other items including a standlet in New York, a cup in Berlin, and two fragmentary cups in London.

He owes much to Corinthian influence, but his work is fully in the Attic tradition. A follower in the stylistic line of the Gorgon Painter and Sophilos, he far surpassed both in ability. He had a happy mastery of drawing and composition, filling his scenes with neat, precise, small, angular, but keen and vivacious figures including gods, goddesses, heroes, men, women, animals, ships, and plant life. The poses of his figures are varied, but convincing. His animals are individualistic, nimble, and slender. His detail and careful labeling of figures is meticulous, while his style is elegant and sure, but subdued. The composition is clear and well-knit. He used incision with great care and employed white for the flesh of females and for fine pattern details. A dance of youths and maidens appears to have been a favorite scene, as it is repeated on several items. He was a true pioneer and brought the narrative style of painting to its apex. His work dates to the second quarter of the sixth century.

The *Painter of Acropolis 606* (a dinos in Athens; see Plate 5b) was a contemporary of Kleitias and also was one of the most able painters of his time. Credited with seven items (all large), he painted in a monumental style unlike Kleitias. A painter of verve, grandeur, and vehemence, he had a gift for vivid drawing, employing bold lines with sensitive incision. His figures are serious, even severe or grim, drawn in clear detail and with robust appreciation of anatomy. Their features are strong and full. Despite use of purple and white, his works are sombre.

Nearchos stands between Kleitias and the Painter of Acropolis 606. Like the former, he could work as a miniaturist, but he also could combine largeness of style with minute detail and gravity of tone as did the Painter of Acropolis 606. He thus combined the delicacy and exquisite detail of the miniaturist with a larger view of life and subtlety of feeling. Nearchos was both potter and painter, and, incidentally, the father of Tleson, a famous potter of cups. He signed as both painter and potter on a kantharos (Athens Acr. 611; see Plate 5c) and is credited with four other items as painter; as potter, he signed six or seven items. Nearchos experimented with a white-background for his black and red tongue bands and is the earliest Attic black-figure painter known to have tried white background.[2] His work dates to the second quarter of the sixth century B.C.

Lydos, whose name is known from his signatures on a dinos (Athens Acr. 607) and on an amphora (Louvre F 29) is one of the three or four great masters of the black-figure technique (see Plate 5d for an example of his work). Though his name means "the Lydian," his work is fully Attic in style. Some 104 items are attributed to him with an additional seventy-eight done in his manner. He may also have been a potter and may have worked with the famous potter Amasis; certainly he worked with the potters Nikosthenes and Kolchos. His works include column-kraters and amphorae as well as small items such as Siana, band, and Proto-A cups.

An innovator, with a flair for the dramatic, Lydos placed his large scale figures continuously around his pots. His humans are firm, solid, and robust with an air of grandeur despite their lively gestures. They are portrayed in a variety of convincing poses and in scenes of action. His animal friezes remind us of the Corinthian, but like his humans, have new solidity and grandeur. His compositions are rhythmical and his drawing elaborate, but broad. He made free use of purple and of beautifully controlled incision. His repertoire of subjects included the deeds of Herakles, heavy-haunched satyrs with incised dotted bodies, scenes from Troy, and horses. He stands close to the Painter of Acropolis 606 and may be dated to the years 560-540 B.C.

The *Painter of Louvre* F 6 (a hydria in Paris) belongs to the same period and was an old-fashioned companion of Lydos. Some 113 works are attributed to him, mostly large items. No potters' names are associated with his work. In some respects he appears to have been a rather mechanical imitator of Lydos, so that his animals are indistinguishable from those of the master though his humans are quite different.

The *Amasis Painter,* so called after the potter Amasis with whom he worked, is credited with 117 items covering a wide range of shapes from amphorae to oinochoai, lekythoi, and cups (see Plate 6a). He learned the elegance of Kleitias, but fell short of the master's ability. He has been criticized as a pure formalist, employing mannered grace and elaboration for its own sake with little concern for underlying form or deeper content. It is true that he was not at his best in attempting the dignified or the sublime, and his efforts in this direction often were empty of meaning. However, his heroic scenes are sometimes cheerfully irreverent and the tipsy gaiety of his Dionysiac scenes with satyrs and maenads show him at his best. Though not an innovator himself, he kept up with change and he was an admirable draftsman with a fine sense for the dramatic. In summary, "his work is always decorative, sometimes a little dull, at his best, enchantingly gay."[3]

His style is polished, simple, symmetrical, light, elegant, precise, and sure. The faces of his figures are strongly accentuated and the bodies well-drawn. Long slim feet and hands with very long, tapering and gesticulating fingers are characteristic of his work. In his early period, the Amasis Painter was conventional and tame, his scenes were crowded with figures and he employed incision only for the most essential details. Later, he became more individualistic, decreasing the number of figures in his scenes to two or three at most and employing incision to a much greater extent. An unusual feature of his work was the outlining of female flesh against the orange-red background instead of covering it in white. His repertoire included scenes from mythology: the Homeric legends, exploits of Herakles, Perseus and the gorgon and, above all, Dionysos and his crew. Though his work covers a long period, from about 550 to 520 B.C., he founded no lasting school.

A very prolific painter of the period and a companion of the Amasis Painter, whom he in no way resembles, was a painter known as the *Affecter* from his archaic affected style (see Plate 6b). He has 119 attributed works, most of which are neckamphorae. These he usually decorated with a secondary scene on the neck, though sometimes this is replaced by a double floral design of palmettes and flowers. He was a mannerist possessing excellent technique, but self-consciously old-fashioned in his work. His compositions are formal decorations, possessing no narrative or special significance. Instead, they are arrangements of stylized, elongated, gawky, but well-dressed and well-drawn figures engaged in lively gesticulations, but strung together with little or no concerted action. His work dates to the third quarter of the sixth century.

A companion of the Affecter, also a mannerist, was a painter known as *Elbows Out* from the affected attitudes of his figures (see Plate 6c in which the figures hold their elbows pointed out). He is credited with a total of forty-three works, including both pots and cups. Like the Affecter, he was an excellent technician but was concerned with obsolete types, neat manikins, and starveling animals and failed to develop coherent subjects.

Another of the lesser, but still important painters of the third quarter of the sixth century is the *Swing Painter,* (named from Boston amphora 98.918; see Plate 6d illustrating his namepiece, a girl in a swing). He was a prolific artist credited with 150 works, mostly amphorae or neck-amphorae. His style is pleasant but uninspired and characterized by careless composition. His figures are simple and expressionless. His drawing is clean, however, and he had a wide range of subjects.

Group E consists of about ninety items, mostly amphorae, one of which (Louvre F 53) bears the signature of Exekias as potter. The vases of this group were painted in the earlier part of the third quarter of the sixth century by painters whose work is closely related (see Plate 7a for an amphora attributed to Group E). One item bears the *kalos* name Stēsias. This is one of the earliest such inscriptions, which began to appear in the mid-sixth century and continued throughout the fifth century. The subjects employed by Group E are often repeated and include the birth of Athena, Theseus and the Minotaur, Herakles and the lion, and Herakles and Geryon.

The greatest master of the black-figure technique is *Exekias*. He signed twelve items, mostly followed by the word *epoiesen* indicating that he was the potter; on two, however, he signed *Exekias egrapse kapoiese,* thus as both potter and painter (on Berlin 1720 and Vatican 344; see Plate 7c; Plates 7b and 7d show other works by Exekias). The only *kalos* name he is known to have employed is Onetorides. In all, twenty-nine items are clearly attributed to

Exekias, though there are several more in his style, some of which may be his work. Most of his attributed items are amphorae, including one prize Panathenaic amphora.

Exekias raised scenes of ordinary life to the level of the heroic, infusing a personal interpretation of events and psychological insight into situations. He was able to impart grave nobility to his figures and tranquility to his scenes.

His composition is strikingly impressive, clean-cut, sophisticated, measured, and neatly integrated with care for balance and subtle relationships. His figures are compact and substantial. The very restraint of their gestures and attitudes adds to their potency in portrayal of mood. There is a wealth of detail especially in the rich ornamentation of cloaks, which are done in infinitely patient incision. He employed equally fine incision on hair, beards, and shield devices. This detail, however, in no way detracts from the rightness of the whole picture, which emerges as one of elegance, force, and quiet distinction. He is equally careful in his inscriptions, the lettering of which is clear, neat, firm, and small. In brief, Exekias is both master draftsman and master painter.

In his early work, he used subsidiary zones of little animals and his style was somewhat conventional, bare, rigid, and close to the work of Group E.

Later, his style became more austere, measured, quiet, and unhurried. Even his Dionysian scenes of this period reflect dignity and sacramental feeling. His heroic scenes beautifully express the tragic grandeur of man — simple, dignified, yet pathetic in the face of the inevitable.

Classic examples of his heroic scenes are his portrayals of Ajax planting his sword in the ground preparatory to killing himself (on an amphora — Boulogne 588), of Achilles and Ajax playing dice during a lull in the battle (an amphora, Vatican 344; see Plate 7c), and of Achilles in the act of thrusting his sword into the breast of the Amazon queen Penthesileia, at the moment when they recognized their mutual love (a neck-amphora, London B 210; see Plate 7d).

Despite Exekias' ability at minute detail, he was not a miniaturist and was at his best on large items. He reminds us of the monumental painting of the Nettos Painter and the Painter of Acropolis 606, from whom he inherited his grave inwardness. Though closest to the latter painter in his battle scenes, Exekias is best in quiet scenes. His work dates to the years 550 to 520 B.C.

Cup Painters

Little Master and Droop Cups ca. 565-510 B.C.

Some twenty-eight personalities have been distinguished as having painted Little Master and Droop cups.[4] Among these are several of the major artists of the period. Thus, Kleitias painted three or four Gordion cups, while Nearchos, Lydos, the Amasis Painter, the Affecter, and Elbows Out each painted a few band-cups and/or lip-cups.[5] Other artists appear to have concentrated on decorating these cups. We shall discuss only two of these specialists.

The *Phrynos Painter,* named after the potter Phrynos with whom he worked, is one of the best of the "Little Masters" (i.e., miniaturists). Only six items are attributed to him, including four cups, but his work is such as to place him among the important painters (see Plate 8a for one of his lip-cups). His short human figures with their large heads are characterized by vigor and movement. His style is terse, finished and living, conveying a sense of narrative power. His incision is firm. He worked in the years ca. 565-525 B.C.

The *Tleson Painter,* named after the potter Tleson, son of Nearchos, was one of the best and most prolific of the Little Masters. (Plate 8b shows a lip-cup by the Tleson Painter, signed by the potter, Tleson.) Of some sixty-three items with which he is credited, fifty-two are lip-cups and ten are band-cups (while about sixty other lip cups or band-cups and one Gordion cup may also be his work). Often his cups have little decoration other than an inscription between the handles. Others have a brief picture of little figures, drawn with grace, precision, and nicety of style on the lip. Still others have a beautiful central medallion inside or combine these inside and outside features. His animals (goats, cocks, swans, sphinxes, lions, and stags) are all highly characteristic of his style. He worked the years ca. 565-525 B.C.

Other painters of Little Master cups who warrant mention include *Sakonides,* the *Taleides Painter* and the *Centaur Painter.*

Proto-A and A Cups ca. 550-500 B.C.

Among seven painters of Proto-A cups, Lydos is the only artist of note (and he is credited with only three cups of this shape).

Some two dozen painters and groups have been identified with decoration of Type A (or eye) cups in black-figure. Among these are Exekias and Sakonides (with one each), the Amasis Painter and the Affecter (with two each), as well as three artists of the late black-figure period, Painter N (with two), the Lysippides Painter (with five), and Psiax (who may have painted one Type A cup).

THE CLOSE OF AN ERA

With the work of the great masters — Lydos, the Amasis Painter and, above all, Exekias — we reach the peak of artistry and craftsmanship in the black-figure technique. That the black-figure technique had any future after Exekias is doubtful at best. In any case, about 530 B.C., from within the Attic workshops came a new influence, which we shall consider in the final chapter. This not only profoundly changed the black-figure technique, but resulted finally in its abandonment.[6]

Notes on V — The Masters of Attic Black-Figure

1. See Arias and Hirmer, *Greek Vase Painting*, Plates 40-46 and pp. 286-92; Beazley, *Dev.*, pp. 20-37; and Cook, *Greek P.P.*, pp. 73-5 for detailed descriptions of this vase.
2. Nearchos tried a white background for a band of tongues on the lip of a kantharos (Athens Acr. 611), Beazley, *Dev.*, p. 40.
3. Robertson, *Greek Painting*, p. 67.
4. These include twenty-four painters and four groups.
5. With the exception of Elbows Out, who currently is credited with about twenty-one of these cups, these artists painted only from one to six Little Master cups each.
6. As noted earlier, Panathenaic amphorae were an exception, being painted in the black-figure technique into the second century B.C.

VI

Attic Black-Figure Following the Masters

LATE BLACK-FIGURE ca. 530-450 B.C.

Sometime about 530 B.C., the red-figure technique was invented, probably by the Andokides Painter. Whereas in the black-figure technique the figures and designs were in black silhouette against the orange-red background of the pot, the red-figure technique involved firing the background black and leaving the figures reserved in the orange-red, with details drawn instead of incised. The new technique offered an opportunity for experimentation and development that was quickly seized by artists of the time.

For a generation after 530 B.C., production of black-figured works increased and the technique maintained acceptable standards, continuing to attract major artists. During this brief period of competition with the red-figure technique, black-figure painters employed fuller composition, and closer groupings of figures and made much use of vines and leaves within the picture. Their figures tended to "act" with expressive facial, arm, and hand gestures. There was a tendency to depict everyday life, often with humor and charm (women weaving or at the fountain, for example), though many scenes continued to be heroic (showing harnessing of chariots, quarrels of heroes, and the like). Efforts were made to render the human body with more coherent anatomy and to show drapery in more natural folds.

A change in women's fashions at this time complicated the problem of portraying drapery. Previously, women had worn a long thick garment, the peplos, which could be depicted plausibly as flat. About 530 B.C., this was replaced by the chiton.[1] A light-weight shift, the chiton required portrayal of fall and folds in any realistic rendering. Black-figure painters sought a solution to this problem by using wavy incised lines, but results were not satisfactory.

A similar problem, realistic portrayal of the himation, or cloak, had been met with almost equally unsuccessful results — black-figure painters using diagonal purple stripes to indicate folds.

Gradually, the inability of the black-figure technique to portray the human body and drapery as convincingly as the new red-figure technique became evident. Incision, at best, was inadequate to portray muscles, tendons, and veins, and its stiffness inhibited infusion of life into the figures. Similarly, incision could not convey the complex folds of drapery. Futhermore, black silhouette bodies were unreal in comparison to the red-figured bodies shown in the new technique. Efforts to solve these problems merely led to fussiness of detail.

By the end of the sixth century, major artists had little interest in black-figured work except on rare occasions. Output and quality declined as the technique came to be used primarily for small vases.

Almost two hundred painters and groups are recognized as falling within the late black-figure category. Some of these are of real importance and others are worthy, at least, of mention; many were hacks, who produced inferior work.

I have divided the late black-figure period (ca. 530-450 B.C.) into two parts, with the dividing line approximately at the end of the sixth century. During the last third of that century there were still competent black-figure artists working with large pots. By the beginning of the sixth century, however, good painters in black-figure were few, and almost all worked with smaller pots. The red-figure technique, in brief, had gained complete dominance for cups and the major shapes.

Period of Competition with Red-Figure ca. 530-500 B.C.

Faced with the challenge of the new technique, some painters ignored it and continued to paint in the black-figure technique, and some experimented in both techniques, while younger paint-ers tended to paint only in the new technique.

Many black-figure painters of the last third of the sixth century were competent artists well established in the old technique who worked with large pot shapes. The less able painters painting only in black-figure worked with small pots. The first red-figure artists worked primarily with amphora shapes and other large pots. Very soon, however, new artists were attracted to kylix shapes, at first, to the Type A or eye-cup, and then, the Type B or one-curve cup. By the end of the sixth century, these kylikes had become by far the most important item of red-figure production. Competition between the two techniques thus pitted the better black-figure painters of large pots against the new red-figure painters of large pots and kylikes.

In this section, we shall discuss the better black-figure artists of the years ca. 530-500 B.C., including one who worked in both techniques and we shall mention some of the red-figure painters who painted at least occasionally in black-figure.

Black-Figure Painters

The *Lysippides Painter's* name is derived from the *kalos* inscription which he employed on a neck-amphora in London (B 211). He is best known, perhaps, for his collaboration with the originator of the red-figure technique, the Andokides Painter, in the production of several "bilingual" vases combining both techniques. Of these, an amphora in Boston (99.538) showing Herakles driving a bull to sacrifice, in red-figure on one side and in black-figure on the other, is perhaps the most dramatic example. At various times, the two painters have been thought to be identical and, in fact, both painted pots made by the potter Andokides.[2] Now, most authorities appear agreed that they were separate artists and that the Lysippides Painter worked only in the black-figure technique.[3] The Lysippides Painter employed not only the *kalos* name from which he derived his sobriquet, but also the name Pordax and the *kalé* name Mnesilla on several of his works. He has twenty-five attributed works; about fifty additional items are at least in his manner. His style is characterized by neat drawing, which is expressive, but tends toward fussiness in composition and detail. An amphora of his in New York (see Plate 10c), showing the procession en route to the deification of Herakles, is typical of the period with its crowded figures and intertwining ivy. This is quite different from the simplicity of Exekias.

The *Antimenes Painter,* so-called after the *kalos* name on one of his hydriai (Leyden XV e 28), also painted only in the black-figure technique. Perhaps a pupil of Lydos, he was one of the chief painters of neck-amphorae and hydriai of the years ca. 530-520 B.C. He has some 158 attributed works including forty-one hydriai and one hundred neck-amphorae; in addition, there are about 113 other items in his manner or related. Besides Antimenes, he also used the *kalos* names Ephiletos and Timotheos and the *kalé* name Sime. His style is similar to that of Psiax, another great painter of the period and like him, he sought charm and humor. Unlike Psiax, whose incision varied from heavy to very fine, the Antimenes Painter used incised lines of equal thickness so that his work is less refined and has fewer details than that of his "brother." A modest painter, his work is broad, natural, buoyant and child-like in its charm. His favorite scene is of the fountain house, which he used on many of his hydriai. These are unusual in their depiction of buildings and their attempts to show perspective. Like others of his time, he crowded his scenes with figures. (See Plate 10d with its numerous figures attending the harnessing of Athena's chariot.)

The *Leagros Group* (ca. 520-510 B.C.) derives its name from frequent use of the *kalos* name Leagros. Who this popular youth was is not known, but he must have been handsome, perhaps a famous athlete or a member of a great family. It has been suggested that he is identical with General Leagros, who was killed in battle in 465 B.C.[4] In any case, this Leagros was praised not only by the Leagros Group, but also by other painters of the time. The Leagros Group comprises numerous interrelated painters, groups and sub-groups. More than 575 items are attributed to the Group, most of them neck-amphorae, but including also many hydriai, lekythoi, amphorae, oinochoai, kraters, and other shapes such as cups and Panathenaic amphorae. (See Plate 11a for a hydria and Plate 15b for a Panathenaic amphora, both attributed to the Leagros Group.) The style of the Group is powerful, vigorous, and sometimes brutal. Composition is bold, often crowded with figures and encumbered with vines and leaves. (Compare Plate 7c with Plate 11a, both showing the same scene. The one by Exekias is simple yet refined, with a wealth of beautiful incision; the other, by the Leagros Group, is crowded and with only cursory incision.) Figures have force, vitality, and intensity and are drawn in free attitudes, making large gestures. There is evident interest in anatomy; muscles are shown, legs often are not in the usual profile view, and poses are frequently complex. Drapery is also complicated. Subjects include harnessing chariot horses, quarrels of heroes, episodes from the life of Herakles, or the Trojan War and other heroic scenes as well as women at fountains.

A modest painter, but still of importance in the late sixth century is the *Rycroft Painter,* who derives his name from an amphora once in the Rycroft collection, now at Northwick. Related to Psiax and possibly a follower of the Lysippides Painter, he has some forty-seven attributed works, mostly amphorae (see Plate 11b). No potter's name is connected with his work. *Kalos* names which he employed include Antimachos, Kar, and Leokrates. His style is neat, firm, precise, and meticulous. His compositions are carefully balanced and usually uncrowded. His figures are drawn with ease and sureness, but are somewhat stiff and rigid. He tended to avoid use of purple and was sparing with incision.

Finally, among these painters mention must be made of two painters connected with the potter Nikosthenes. Nikosthenes never signed as painter, though as noted earlier, he signed many items as potter.

The "painter of the neck-amphora with the signature of Nikosthenes, No. B 295 in the British Museum," otherwise known as the *BMN Painter,* is credited with twenty-three items in all, including nine neck-amphorae of various sizes (see Plate 11c). His drawing is neat, lively, and pleasant, but undistinguished.

The *Painter N* was more prolific, with seventy-eight Nikosthenic neck-amphorae among his eighty-six clearly attributed items, and he may have painted another fourteen of these special amphorae. His output, however, is not matched by his skill in painting. His style is conventional and cursory at best, and often is slovenly. He had an unhappy penchant for running his drawings over the two raised fillets girdling the upper belly of Nikosthenic amphorae.

Both the BMN Painter and Painter N straddle the division between mature and late black-figure, but the quality of their work seems to place them more appropriately in the latter period.

Painters in Both Techniques

During the years after the invention of the red-figure technique, several of the major painters worked in both black-figure and red-figure.

Psiax was one of the major artists working in both techniques in the years ca. 530-510 B.C. Though primarily a black-figure paint-er, his name is known from *egrapsen* signatures on two red-figured alabastra (Karlsruhe 242 and *Odessa Zap.* Od. 17 pl.2). Formerly, he was known as the "Menon Painter" from the potter, Menon, with whom he worked in red-figure (he also worked in red-figure with the potters Hilinos and Andokides). In black-figure, he is known to have worked only with the potter Andokides. On his black-figured work, he used the *kalos* names Aischis, Hippokrates, Karystios, and Simikrion. In addition to normal black-figure and red-figure,

Psiax experimented with black silhouette on a special coral red, with white background and with the Six's technique.

Close in style to the Antimenes Painter, probably a pupil of the Amasis Painter and perhaps the teacher of the great red-figure artist Phintias, Psiax stands between the two major techniques. He was at his best, however, in black-figure. He painted vases of all sizes from amphorae to alabastra and is credited with twenty-five black-figured items in all (see Plate 11d), plus perhaps two others with nine near his style; in red-figure, he has thirteen attributed items. It appears that he liked small vases best and was by nature a miniaturist, seeking charm and humor. His drafting is delicate with dainty incision varying from fine to very fine. His style is charming but meticulous, with a wealth of highly finished detail. He had a gift for portrayal of character and was fairly accurate in his depiction of anatomy. He was fond of showing the details of the outlandish dress (Scythian and Thracian) affected by Attic cavalry and archers of the period. Other of his favorite depictions include horses and Dionysiac scenes.

The other better painters of the period are primarily red-figure artists. Some of these worked occasionally in black-figure. *Oltos,* for example, with 157 attributed red-figure items, painted the interiors of at least twenty-four eye-cups and one Type A cup in black-figure. Other artists painting in both techniques include *Epiktetos,* the *Dikaios Painter, Paseas,* and *Euphronios.* The latter, in addition to twenty-five attributed red-figure works, is credited with a Panathenaic amphora (Athens Acr. 931), which may have been a prize vase. He may be the first of the great red-figure artists commissioned to paint one of these special black-figure items.

Thus, for a little more than a generation, there were important artists working in both techniques and standards in each were such as to provide competition on a more or less even basis.

Decline of Black-Figure ca. 500-450 B.C.

By the end of the sixth century, most good painters were working in the red-figure technique. With perhaps two exceptions, red-figure artists of ability painted only rarely in black-figure and then usually only when commissioned to paint Panathenaic amphorae.

In this section, we shall mention very briefly the red-figure artists who occasionally painted in black-figure and then turn our attention to a few of the many painters of small pots who worked in black-figure until extinction of the technique about mid-fifth century.

Red-Figure Artists Painting in Black-Figure

The *Nikoxenos Painter,* the *Eucharides Painter* and the *Bowdoin Painter* appear to be the only artists of the fifth century who worked regularly in both techniques.[5] Others including the *Kleophrades, Berlin, Achilles, Providence,* and *Aegisthus* painters worked only occasionally in black-figure and then usually on Panathenaic amphorae. (See Plate 15c for a Panathenaic prize amphora by the Kleophrades Painter.)[6]

Black-Figure Painters

The best of the black-figure painters of the fifth century cannot be compared to the better sixth century artists of that technique and would not even have been mentioned in previous chapters. Our story, however, would not be complete without mention of some of them and illustration of their works. (Comparison of the vases pictured in Plates 12c through 14c with vases shown in preceding plates will illustrate vividly the decline in composition and workmanship.)

These late painters concentrated on small pots more or less by default. Throughout the era of the black-figure technique, lekythoi, oinochoai, and other small pots had been produced in large quantities, but the better artists had avoided the shapes. Red-figure artists also concentrated on kylikes and large pots, leaving the smaller pots to less talented painters.

Most of the painters of small pots continued to employ black-figure silhouette figures against an orange-red background. In the very late sixth century, however, some of them began to employ a white background on small pots, especially lekythoi. A little later, a few experimented with outline or semi-outline drawing, using either full-strength or dilute lines. These experiments failed to have much importance in the black-figure technique, but presaged developments of importance in the red-figure technique.[7]

The *Gela Painter* (most of his works were found at Gela, in Sicily) painted in the normal black-figure technique against an orange-red background. He was prolific, with 274 attributed items, of which 230 are lekythoi and thirty-four are oinochoai. He seems to have little else to recommend him. He had not much feeling for proportion and his groups are often mere juxtapositions of figures, which are thick-set, stiff, short-legged, long-nosed and have "skipper" beards (see Plate 12c). He is typical of the late black-figure painters in his poor composition and drafting.

The *Cactus Painter* (his palmettes and shoulder decorations have cactus-like spiky buds), though credited with only six lekythoi and one oinochoe, warrants mention for his extremely delicate style. His figures are refined and drawn with beautiful incision, yet despite his precision, his work blends into an harmonious whole. He does not appear to have tried the white background.

The *Edinburgh Painter* (named after two lekythoi in the Edinburgh Museum 1872.23.12 and L224.379) painted only twenty-five lekythoi, out of a total of sixty-five attributed works, yet is ranked as the chief painter of this shape at the end of the sixth century.[8] He appears to have been one of the first to apply a creamy-white background slip to lekythoi. In his early work, he used white for the flesh of women, but later abandoned this for black, as did most of his followers. He tended to paint large, rather archaic looking figures with "on-lookers" wearing "Robin Hood" caps. His style was simple and clear. His favorite depictions were of mythological scenes, often featuring chariots. Sure, but somewhat thick incision characterizes his style (see Plate 12d). The Athena and Theseus painters carried on his work.

The *Marathon Painter's* chief claim to fame appears to lie in the fact that he painted the better lekythoi found in the tumulus erected in honor of the Athenian dead after the battle of Marathon in 490 B.C. All of his attributed thirty-seven items are lekythoi (see Plate 13a). He used both red and white backgrounds, often on the same vase, and tended to crowd available free space with filling ornaments. His humans usually are heavily draped and his horses tend to have "wooden" manes, indicating a lack of interest in anatomy.

The *Sappho Painter,* named after his depiction of the poetess on a kalpis (Goluchow 32), has twenty-two attributed items (see Plate 13b), mostly lekythoi, one of which is in semi-outline. A good painter, his compositions have unity, though he tended to leave shields and helmets lying about the scene. He often painted spritely people carrying pets, such as owls, fish, or dolphins, and frequently included horses and chariots. In addition to his normal black-figured work, he also did several vases in the Six's technique and one in semi-outline on a white background.

Working closely with the Sappho Painter was the *Diosphos Painter* whose name is derived from the inscription *Kalos Diosphos Hera* on a small neck-amphora in Paris (Cab. Med. 219); he also appears to have used the *kalos* names Kallikrates and Sonantios. The Diosphos Painter and the Sappho Painter have much in common, yet differ in several respects. Thus, the Diosphos painter tended to concentrate on tall slim lekythoi (most of his sixty-eight attributed works are lekythoi; see Plate 13c), whereas the Sappho Painter concentrated on large bulky lekythoi.

The Diosphos Painter was more original and varied in his scenes and more of a decorator than painter, whereas the Sappho Painter's work, while less original, had more unity. The Diosphos Painter also depicted people with pets, but they resemble children playing. Like the Sappho Painter, he left shields and helmets lying around and often drew horses and chariots. Inscriptions are more frequent on the work of the Diosphos Painter than on that of the Sappho Painter. The Diosphos Painter was better than his "brother" in the Six's technique and worked more often in semi-outline against a white background.

Among painters of skyphoi, the *Theseus Painter* (named after his favorite subject) stands out. He is credited with forty-eight of these cups among a total of ninety-four works. One of the really sound painters among many hacks of his time, he employed incision with long flowing strokes, frequently combining various features in one line. He often employed yellow for hair and was lavish in his use of white. A peculiarity of his work is the drawing of a forward-falling zig-zag on the lower edges of chitons. He liked to depict trees and weird monsters. (See the strange seahorse on his skyphos pictured in Plate 13d.)

Related to the Theseus Painter, and probably identical with the red-figure Bowdoin Painter, is the *Athena Painter* (named from his frequent depictions of the goddess; see Plate 14a). All but one of his fifty-seven attributed black-figure works are lekythoi. His figures have over-refined faces so that they appear small, sharp, or even spectral. In general, his incision is hard, but on animals and birds it is very fine, giving them a hairy or feathery appearance. His scenes seldom have unity.

A painter who depicted a sphinx with its victim, probably Haimon, the son of King Kreon of Thebes, on four items, is known as the *Haimon Painter*. The twenty-nine lekythoi attributed to him are only a few among the some 750 lekythoi and many other shapes assigned to the Haimon Group.[9] His figures have long faces with scanty indication of eyes and mouth, and bodies which are attenuated and meager (see Plate 14b). His horses have long, untidy, forward-falling manes and usually lift both front feet in the air. About all his figures there is an air of vagueness.

With the *Emporion Painter* (four of his alabastra were found at the site of ancient Emporium in Spain), we come near the end of black-figured work. He is credited with twenty-five lekythoi and twenty alabastra; some of his lekythoi are of the ungainly "chimney type," typical of the very late period (see Plate 14c). His work is characterized by dull black firing and use of filling ornaments. His figures often have fringed hair and "flat-iron" feet. Tiny waves that look like drops on the lower edges of garments also are characteristic of his work. His favorite scenes include youths, barbarians, dancers, and flying women.

The last black-figure painter of any possible note is the *Beldam Painter,* so-called from the hag pictured on one of his large lekythoi (Athens 1129). His attributed thirty-seven works are all lekythoi. He featured unusual scenes, often of torture, and his people have queer stunted hands with thumbs that stick out. His compositions, however, have unity and he employed fine incision. He worked in the years ca. 480 to 450 B.C.

With the Beldam Painter we have reached the end of the Attic black-figure technique except as it persisted in Panathenaic amphorae. In covering the decline of the technique from ca. 500 to 450 B.C., mention has been made of painters of lekythoi, skyphoi, oinochoai, and other small shapes. There were, of course, painters of cups and large items, but none that appear worthy of mention. For the great artists of these years one must turn to red-figured work.

RETROSPECT

In following the development of the Attic black-figure technique, we have witnessed an interesting evolution. We traced the origins of Attic pottery from the years following the Dorian invasion, which forced collapse of the Mycenaean civilization. That Athens itself was not captured and reduced may account for its preeminence in the production of Protogeometric and Geometric pottery. In any case, this sophisticated but highly intricate and abstract art appears to have reflected the austerity of life occasioned by the disturbed political, economic, and social conditions of that period, often referred to as the "Dark Ages."

Break with the Geometric style followed the great wave of Greek colonization in the eighth century B.C. This swept not only along the previously Greek-colonized shores of Anatolia, but also to Italy, Sicily, Gaul, the Pillars of Hercules, and back along the North African littoral to Egypt and the lands of the Near East. Colonial relations and trade with the already-civilized East were reflected in Greek pottery by new designs, new motifs, and relaxation of style. Proto-Corinthian and Corinthian pottery, early products of this orientalizing influence, were of such quality as to enable Corinth to become the ceramic center of the Mediterranean world. In Attica, the new ideas led to a local development, the Proto-Attic style, which was boisterous and crude yet powerful in its massiveness.

The legal and administrative reforms of Solon (ca. 594 B.C.) may have encouraged potters and painters to move from Corinth to Athens. At least, these reforms created a better climate for industry. The Corinthian influence tamed the exuberance of the Proto-Attic style resulting, at first, in rather abject imitation of Corinthian shapes and painting styles, but soon, in stimulation of new concepts of composition, style, and design. By ca. 550 B.C., Athens had successfully challenged and eliminated Corinth as the pottery capital of the ancient world.

That the tenure of the "tyrant" Peisistratos (ca. 561-527 B.C., with interruptions) coincided with the period of the great masters of the black-figure technique is not surprising. The rule of Peisistratos was characterized by encouragement of industry, trade, intellectual life, and the arts. It was a period of prosperity in Attica, when the upper classes had the wealth to acquire works of art and the culture to appreciate them. In these years, black-figure artists attained complete mastery of their medium in what might be called the "classic" moment in the black-figure technique. In such works as Exekias' Vatican vase, we can see embodied those qualities of simplicity, symmetry, economy of line, precision of detail, naturalism, and humanism which characterize the best of all Greek art.

As we have seen, decline of the black-figure technique resulted from two factors: first, exhaustion of its possibilities by the great masters and, secondly, introduction of the red-figure technique. The latter development offered new avenues of expression leading the better new artists to choose it in preference to the old technique during the closing years of the sixth century. What followed in black-figure after the great masters was merely an unhappy epilogue.

The glories of Marathon, Salamis, and Plataea failed to have any revitalizing effect on late black-figure painters. For a reflection in painted pottery of the exhilaration of these events, one must examine works in the red-figure technique.

Notes on VI — Attic Black-Figure Following the Masters

1. A vase portraying a woman wearing a chiton thus cannot antedate 530 B.C. by more than a few years at most.

2. This has led to confusion as to the number of works attributed to these two painters and the use of *kalos* names.

3. See Beazley, *ABV*, p. 254, and Dietrich von Bothmer, "Andokides the Potter and the Andokides Painter," *Bulletin* of the Metropolitan Museum of Art (New York: February 1966), p. 208.

4. Richter, *Survey*, p. 45.

5. If, in fact, the red-figure Bowdoin Painter and the black-figure Athena Painter are identical, as is generally supposed.

6. In addition to those listed, mention may be made of Douris and the Troilos Painter, with one black-figure item attributed to each.

7. In the 460s B.C., lekythoi suddenly became popular in both red-figured and white-ground work. Adaptation about this time of the form painted on white ground to funerary use added impetus to this trend. As a result, for a short time major painters worked with the form, specialists in white-ground work appeared, and the white-ground lekythos became one of the chief items of production. See Richter, *Survey*, p. 75.

8. Interestingly, it appears that the Nolan amphora, so popular later in red-figure, may have been invented in his workshop.

9. This comprises many vases similar in style to the work of the Haiman Painter.

SUMMARY CHART
(Dates approximate)

MAJOR PERIODS	SUB-PERIODS	STYLISTIC AND OTHER DEVELOPMENTS	MAJOR PAINTERS	MAJOR POTTERS	SHAPES
PROTO-ATTIC 710-610 B.C.	Early Proto-Attic 710-680	Orientalizing influence on old Geometric tradition; introduction of plants, animals; flowing lines; outline drawing predominant.	Analatos P. P. of Ram Jug P. of N.Y. Nessos Amphora	None identified by name	Large shapes were most important: large neck-amphora, kotyle-krater, etc. Smaller shapes also, i.e., globular oinochoe, stemmed bowl, mug, and skyphos.
	Black and White Style 680-650	Silhouette and incision introduced early in 7th century. White introduced in mid-7th cent. Red introduced in third quarter 7th cent.	Nettos P.		Trend towards slimmer pots with slurred angles.
	Late Proto-Attic 650-610	Proto-Attic tradition combined with Corinthian influence. Silhouettes. Development of orange background and a better black for silhouettes.	Piraeus P. Potos P. Gorgon P. Sophilos		One-piece amphora Type B introduced.
	Earliest Black Figure 625-600	Corinthian influence dominant.	Castellani P. Timiades P.	Sophilos	Borrowings from Corinth included lekanis, plate, pyxis, aryballos, alabastron, column-krater, hydria, and lekythos (round and oval). New shapes and types were: Panel amphora 600-550 Tyrrhenian amphora 600-550 Slender-neck amphora 575-550 Komast cups 585-570 Siana cups 575-550
	Early Black-Figure 610-550	Animal Style 625-550. Major trends in 560s and 550s: Monumental Works Mass Production Miniatures Narrative	KX and Ky Painters C and Heidelberg Painters Goltyr. P. Kleitas P. of Acropolis 606	Cheiron Ergotimos	Volute-krater 560 to red-figure Panathanaic amphora 565 to second century
ATTIC BLACK-FIGURE 610-450 B.C.	Mature Black-Figure 570-525	Human Style 550-450 Trends after 550s: Single large composition Mannerists First appearance of *kalos* names. Culmination of black-figure technique.	Nearchos Lydos P. of Louvre F6 Phrynos P. Tleson P. Sakonides Taleides P. Affecter Elbows Out Group E Exekias Amasis P. Swing P.	Nearchos Lydos Hermogenes Phrynos Tleson Eucheiros Taleides Charitaios Xenokles Exekias Amasis	Early shoulder lekythos Little Master cups Lip-cups 565-535 Band-cups 550-520 Droop cups 560-510 One-piece amphora Type A 550 to red-figure One-piece amphora Type C 550 to red-figure Type A or eye-kylix 540-500 Stamnos, pelike, kalpis, and calyx-krater 530 to red-figure
	Late Black-Figure 530-450	Introduction of red-figure 530. Competition with red-figure 530-500. *Kalos* and *kalé* names fairly common. Decline of black-figure 500-450.	Lysippidos P. Psiax Antimenes P. Leagros Group Gela P. Edinburgh P. Marathon P. Sappho P. Diosphos P.	Nikosthenes Andokides Pamphaios	Cylindrical shoulder lekythos 530 Nikosthenic amphora 525-500 Standard lekythos 500 to red-figure Type B and C kylikes 500 to red-figure Small items predominant: lekythos, oinochoe, and skyphos. Best large items and cups done in red-figure. Chimney lekythos 470-450

141

APPENDIX I

NOTES ON ATTRIBUTIONS

1. Throughout this book, I have relied primarily on Sir John Davidson Beazley's *Attic Black-figure Vase Painters* and his *Attic Red-figure Vase Painters* as modified by his *Paralipomena* in attributing vases to various painters and groups. Beazley is extremely careful to differentiate as among vases painted by a painter, in his manner, in imitation, by his followers, in his workshop, school, circle or group, under his influence or akin to his work. I have retained a clear distinction between items actually attributed to a painter and those otherwise related to him. I have included reference to works in a painter's manner, etc., only if they appear to be very close to the painter's own work. Serious students should refer to Beazley's works for these distinctions.

2. Attribution of a particular number of items to a given painter does not mean:
   a. that this number is all that he painted. (Obviously, the painter did other work, some of which has been attributed to him by other authorities and much of which has never been found.) The number refers only to those which have been found and attributed by Beazley;
   b. that all are complete items. If the shape of the fragment permits identification of the original shape, it is so listed; thus, an identifiable cup fragment is listed as a cup.

142

APPENDIX II

POTTERS OF BLACK-FIGURED VASES

For the names of potters of black-figured vases who signed their work, I am indebted to Sir John Davidson Beazley's *Attic Black-figure Vase Painters* as amended by his *Paralipomena*.

The practice of signing by potters was not consistent and was not practiced by all potters. Many of the best craftsmen never signed their works, while others signed sporadically, sometimes signing an indifferent item while failing to sign a masterpiece. (In this connection, see J. V. Noble, *The Technique of Attic Painted Pottery,* p. xii).

BLACK-FIGURE POTTERS

Potter's Name	Association, Painter(s)	Items
1. Aischines	Unattributed	base (?)
2. Amasis	Amasis Painter	2 neck-amphorae; 4 oinochoai; 1 cup (similar to Type A)
	Probably Amasis P.	1 beaker, 1 fragment
	Lydos (?)	1 amphora; 1 psykter-amphora
3. Anakles	Unattributed	3 lip-cups; 1 band-cup
4. Andokides*	Psiax	2 amphorae
	Lysippides Painter	1 bilingual cup
	Unattributed	1 amphora
5. Antidoros	Unattributed	2 Droop cups; possibly 1 Droop cup
6. Archeneides	Unattributed	1 lip-cup
7. Archikles	Unattributed	1 lip-Gordion cup; 2 band-cups
8. Bakchios	Unattributed	2 Panathenaic amphorae
9. Charinos	Unattributed	1 oinochoe
10. Charitaios	Charitaios Painter	1 hydria
	Unattributed	2 lip-cups
11. Cheiron	Manner of the C Painter	1 Siana cup
12. Chiron (may be same as Cheiron)	Unattributed	1 Little Master cup
13. Epitimos	Akin to earliest Lydos	1 lip-cup
	Epitimos Painter	1 lip-cup
14. Ergoteles (son of Nearchos)	Unattributed	1 lip-cup, 1 Little Master cup; 1 cup fragment, with Erg...
15. Ergotimos	Kleitias	1 volute-krater; 1 skyphos or kantharos 1 Sosian-type standlet; 3 Gordion cups
	Unattributed	1 footless cup
16. Eucheiros, son of Ergotimos	Sakonides	1 lip-cup
	Unattributed	2 lip-cups; 1 Little Master cup
17. Eucheiros (?), a son of Ergotimos	Unattributed	1 lip-cup or Gordian cup
18. Eucheiros, son of	Unattributed	1 lip-cup
19. Exekias	Exekias	2 neck-amphorae; 1 amphora, Type A; 1 dinos; 1 Type A kylix

144

	Unattributed	4 lip-cups; 1 unknown shape; 1 amphora or neck-amphora
	Group E	1 amphora, Type B
20. Gageos	Unattributed	1 lip-cup
21. Glaukytes	Unattributed	2 band-cups; 1 lip-cup; 1 band-cup fragment; possibly 1 band-cup
22. Hermogenes	Unattributed (by various hands)	9 lip-cups
	Unattributed	7 band-cups
	Unattributed (no figure work)	7 lip-cups; 1 special cup; 1 band-cup; 4 skyphoi; possibly 1 cup, 1 skyphos, and several cup fragments
23. Hischylos**	Unattributed (probably same hand)	2 band-cups
	Unattributed	1 column-krater
24. Ismenos	Unattributed	1 skyphos fragment
25. Kaulos	Sakonides	1 band-cup
26. Kittos	Unattributed	1 Panathenaic amphora
27. Kleimachos	Unattributed	1 neck-amphora
28. Klitomenes (or Kritomenes)	Unattributed	1 skyphos
29. Kolchos	Lydos	1 oinochoe
30. Kr. . .es (Kares?)	Unattributed	1 lip-cup; possibly 1 globular vase
31. Kriton	Kriton Group	1 olpe
32. Lydos (?)	Lydos	1 dinos
33. Lysiades	Unattributed	1 kothon; plus possibly others without signatures
34. Lysias	Kriton Group	1 olpe
35. M. . .	Unattributed	1 votive shield
36. Mnesiades	Unattributed	1 fragment (hydria?)
37. Mnes. . .	Manner of the Princeton Painter, but not clear whether inscription is a *kalos* name or potter's signature, possibly Mnesiades, but different lettering	1 neck-amphora fragment
38. Myspios	Unattributed	1 lip-cup

39. Neandros	Unattributed	2 lip-cups; 1 band-cup; possibly 1 pyxis lid and 2 Little Master cups with partial signatures which may be Sondros
40. Nearchos	Nearchos (signature missing)	1 kantharos; 1 lip-cup 1 kantharos; 1 aryballos; 1 plaque; 1 lip-cup; possibly 1 cup-bowl
41. Nikos-thenes**	See entry 70	
42. Oikopheles	Oikopheles	1 small standed dish
43. Pamphaios**	Euphiletos Painter Unattributed	2 hydriai 8 cups
44. Phrynos	Phrynos Painter possibly Phrynos P.	1 lip-cup 1 lip-cup
45. Polypous (signature or *kalos* inscription)	Unattributed	1 lip-cup
46. Priapos	Kriton Group Unattributed	1 oinochoe 1 aryballos; 2 skyphoi; 1 Little Master cup
47. Proklees	Unattributed	1 sculptured aryballos
48. (Ps)oleas	Recalls C Painter	1 cup fragment(?)
49. Pyrrhos (may be Pyrrhias; not clear whether potter's signature or *kalos* name)	Unattributed	1 lip-cup
50. Sakonides (?)	Unattributed	1 band-cup (incised signature)
51. Salax	Unattributed	1 plate
52. Smikrion may be a *kalos* inscription	Unattributed	1 band-cup
53. Sokles	Unattributed	2 Gordion cups; 1 lip-cup; 3 band-cups
54. Sondros (see Neandros)	Unattributed	3 Gordion cups; 3 Gordion or Little Master cups; 1 Gordion or lip-cup
55. Sophilos	Sophilos	2 dinoi; 1 krater (?)
56. Sosimos	Unattributed	1 phiale
57. Sotes	Paideros	1 plate
58. Taleides	Taleides Painter	1 amphora; 1 loutrophoros; 1 oinochoe; 1 lekythos (?), 1 Siana cup; 5 lip-cups; 1 fragment
	similar to Taleides P.	1 oinochoe
	Unattributed	1 oinochoe; 1 band-cup; possibly 1 lip- or band-cup

59. Teisias (?) (may be *kalos* name)	Unattributed	1 lip-cup
60. Teles (may be Telesias)	Unattributed	1 Little Master cup
61. Theozotos	Unattributed	1 kyathoid vase
62. Thrax	Unattributed	1 band-cup; 1 skyphos
63. Thypheithides	Unattributed	1 Little Master cup
64. Timagoras	Taleides Painter	2 hydriai
65. Timenor	Unattributed	1 Type A kylix
66. Tlempolemos	Sakonides	1 lip-cup
	near the Taleides P.	1 lip-cup
	Unattributed	1 band-cup
67. Tleson, son of Nearchos**	See entry 71	
68. Tychios	Unattributed	1 hydria
69. Xenokles	Xenokles Painter	8 lip-cups
	influenced by C Painter	1 lip-cup
	comparable	1 lip-cup
	Kleisophos Painter	1 oinochoe
	Unattributed	9 lip-cups; 1 lip- or band-cup; 7 band-cups; possibly 1 lip- or band-cup

	Associated Painters	*Number of Items*
70. Nikosthenes***	Painter N	85
	near Painter N	21
	Six's technique	1
	BMN Painter	18
	near BMN Painter	3
	related to BMN Painter	1
	Lydos	5
	Painter of Louvre F117	2
	Miscellaneous	43
	Total	179

70. Nikosthenes
    (cont.)

Types of Items	Signed	Unsigned	Total
Nikosthenic neck amphorae	76	15	91
Other neck amphorae	2	17	19
Amphorae, Typè B	1	2	3
Cups	28	11	39
Kyathoi	4	1	5
Oinochoai	3	4	7
Skyphoi	3	1	4
Phialai	3	—	3
Lids	2	—	2
Plates	—	1	1
Hydria	—	1	1
Pyxides	1	1	2
Volute-Krater	1	—	1
Frag. Unidentified	1	—	1
Totals	125	54	179

71 Tleson, son
   of Nearchos†

Associated Painters	Number of Items
Tleson Painter	50
possibly Tleson P.	4
style of Tleson P.	54
Unattributed	1
Total	109

Types of Items	Signed	Possibly Signed	Unsigned	Total
Lip-cups	56	12	6	74
Band-cups	4	1	6	11
Lip- or band-cups	21	—	—	21
Gordion cups	1	—	—	1
Pyxis	—	—	1	1
Shape unknown	1	—	—	1
Totals	83	13	13	109

   * Also potted red-figured items for the Andokides Painter and Epiktetos
  ** Also a potter of red-figured items
 *** See *ABV*, pp. 216-235 for details
   † See *ABV*, pp. 178-183 for details

APPENDIX III

KALOS AND KALÉ NAMES

Again, I am indebted to Sir John Davidson Beazley's *Attic Black-figure Vase Painters* and his *Paralipomena* for the *kalos* and *kalé* names employed by black-figure painters.

I have separated the list into (1) names which can be associated directly or indirectly with some painter or group and (2) those which are unattributed to any painter or group.

ATTRIBUTED KALOS AND KALÉ NAMES

Kalos (masculine) Names	Painter Using Name or Other Identification
Aischis	Psiax
Andokides	Taleides P.
Antimachos	Rycroft P.
Antimenes	Antimenes P.
Archias	Leagros Group or near it
Aristomenes	near Group E and associated with work of potter Mnesiades
Automenes	manner of Lysippides P. and near Mastos P.
Chaireleos	Kephisophon P.
Choiros	related to the Lysippides P.
Diodotos	Edinburgh P.
Dorotheos	related to Group of London B 632
Elparetos	related to the Lysippides P.
Erasippos	see Heraspos
Euphiletos	Euphiletos P. Antimenes P.
Heraspos (may actually mean Erasippos)	manner of Lysippides P.
Hipparchos	associated with *kalos* name Dorotheos
Hippokl (es?) or Hippokl (eides)	near Exekias or Group E
Hippokrates	Psiax (bilingual) Three-line Group manner of Lysippides P.
Kallias	Three-line Group (associated with potter Taleides)
Kallikrates	Diosphos P.
Kar	Rycroft P.
Karystios	Psiax
Kephisophon	Kephisophon P.
Kleitarchos	Taleides P.
Leagros	Painter A Group of Vatican 424 Leagros Group generally
Leokrates	Rycroft P.
Lykos II	Edinburgh P.
Lysippides	Lysippides P. Group of London B 339

150

Memnon	related to Group of London B 632
Mnes . . . ? (doubtful that this is a *kalos* inscription)	manner of Princeton P.
Mynnichos	Priam P.
Neokleides	Taleides P.
Nikesippos	Nikesippos Group
Nikias	Priam P.
Nikolas	related to Group of London B 632
Nikostratos	akin to vases in manner of the Lysippides P.
Olympiodoros	Leagros Group
Onetor	Edinburgh P.
Onetorides	Exekias
	Princeton P.
	Three-line Group
	Mastos Painter
	Nikesippos Group
Orthagoras	Three-line Group
Pasikles	Pasikles P.
Pedieus	Three-line Group
Philon	Philon P.
	Three-line Group
	manner of the Lysippides P.
Pordax	Lysippides P.
Proxenides	In Six's technique, related to Sappho and Diosphos painters
Pyrgion	On band-cup with signature Sakonides incised
Sonantios	Diosphos P.
Smikrion	Psiax
Sostratos	Manner of the Acheloos P.
Stēsias	Group E
Stesileos	somewhat recalls the style of the Rycroft P.
Stroibos	Sakonides
Telenikos	probably Sappho P.
Teles	Priam P.
Timokleides	Taleides P.
Timotheos	Antimenes P.
	Long-nose P.

151

Kalé (feminine)
 Names

Hegesilla	maner of Antimenes P.
Kallippe	manner of Antimenes P.
Korinno	A.D. Painter
Korone	near the Sappho P.
Mnesilla	Lysippides P. and manner of the Antimenes P.
Rhodopis (?)	A.D. Painter (*kalé* omitted)
Rhodon	Group of London B 339 (Rhodon also found without *kalé*)
Sime	Antimenes P.

OTHER KALOS AND KALÉ NAMES, NOT ATTRIBUTED

Kalos (masculine) Names

Ainios	Associated with *kalos* name Chares
Andrias	(lip-cup)
Athen . . .	(Type C cup)
Chairias	
Chares	(or Chairias?)
	Associated with *kalos* name Ainios
Echekles	
Eumares	Associated with work of potter Salax
Euphamidas	
Hippokritos	(band-cup)
	Associated with work of potter Glaukytes
Hippon	
Hipponikos	
Hippoteles	(lip-cup)
Kallixenos (?)	(Not clear that is a *kalos* name)
Lykis	(lip-cup)
Lykos (?)	(earlier than *kalos* name Lykos used by Edinburgh P.)
Mys	(on oinochoe of Keyside Class — see ABV p. 426)
Nikon	
Nikosthenes	(on pyxis of Nikosthenic shape)

152

Peisandrides	
Polykles	
Polypous	(Not clear whether a signature or a *kalos* inscription)
Pyrrhos or Pyrrhias	(lip-cup)
Pythis	
Pythokles	
Simiades	(Probably was accompanied by *kalos*)
Teisias (?)	(lip-cup fragment) not clear whether *kalos* name or signature
Theognis	(lip-cup)
. . . bis	(fragment of Nikosthenes pyxis?)
. . . ias	(perhaps Charias?)

Kalé (feminine) Names

Anthyle	period of Lysippides and Antimenes painters, also found as a graffito, dating to the middle of the third quarter of the sixth century.
Anthylla	
Kallis	
Kallistanthe	
Melo	
Myrtale	
Myrte (?)	

APPENDIX IV

PAINTERS OF PANATHENAIC AMPHORAE

This appendix also is based on Sir John D. Beazley's *Attic Black-figure Vase Painters* as well as on his *Attic Red-figure Vase Painters* as amended by his *Paralipomena*.

154

PAINTERS OF PANATHENAIC AMPHORAE

Painter or Group	Number of Items Attributed		
	Prize	Possibly Prize	Amphorae of P.A. Shape
Black-figure Painters			
Manner of Gorgon P.	—	—	2 small amphoriskoi
Boeotian imitations	—	—	2 small amphoriskoi
P. of Boston CA	—	—	1
Gr. of Vatican G52	—	—	1
Near P. of Acropolis 606	—	—	1
P. of London B76	—	—	1
Burgon Gr.	1	—	1
P. of Boston 08.291	—	—	1 amphoriskos
Lydos	1	1	—
Near Lydos	—	1	—
Gr. of Vatican 347	—	—	2
Group E	—	1	—
Exekias	1	—	—
Manner of Exekias	1	—	—
Manner of Lysippides P.	—	—	1
Mastos P.	2	1	—
Antimenes P.	—	4	—
Manner of Antimenes P.	—	1	—
Related to Antimenes P.	1	—	—
Eye-Siren Gr.	—	2	—
P. of Boulogne 441	1	—	—
Comparable to above	1	—	—
P. of Warsaw Panathenaic	2	—	—
Princeton P.	—	—	2
Manner of Princeton P.	—	2	—
Swing P.	—	—	4
P. of Louvre F51	—	2	—
Bucci P.	—	—	1
Euphiletos P.	10	2	2
P. of Wurzburg 173	—	1	—
P. of Tarquinia RC 6847	—	—	1
P. of Oxford 218 B	—	—	4 small
Rather like the P. of Oxford 218 B	—	—	15 small
P. of Brunswick 218	—	—	1 small
Michigan P.	3	—	—
Recalling Michigan P.	—	1	—
Leagros Gr. (unattrib.spec.)	3	4	1
Gr. of Wurzburg 210	—	—	2
Acheloos P.	—	—	2
P. of Munich 1519	—	3	—
P. of London B 495	—	—	1 small

Red-figure Painters*

Euphronios	—	1
Kleophrades P.	12	5
Near the Kleophrades P.	7	2
Berlin P.	8	8
Probably by the Berlin P.	1	—
Near the Berlin P.	2	—
Eucharides P.	4	17
By or near Eucharides P.	—	1
Aegisthus P.	1	—
Providence P.	—	2
Achilles P.	6	—
Probably by Achilles P.	—	1

**Apparent Specialists
in Panathenaic Amphorae**

Gr. of Copenhagen 99	1	2	—
Sikelos	1	2	—*egrapsen* on Naples inv. 11.28.48
Gr. of Vatican G23	2	2	—plus 3 b-f neck amphorae
Near Gr. of Vatican G23	—	1	—
P. of Berlin 1833	2	—	—
Near P. of Berlin 1833	2	—	—
Gr. of Compiegne 985	1	2	—
Comparable	—	3	—
Robinson Gr.	5	—	—
Connected to Robinson Gr.	2	—	—
Kuban Gr.	6	—	—
Near or akin to Kuban Gr.	4	—	—
Comparable	—	1	—
Hildesheim Gr.	2	—	—
Asteios Gr.	3	—	—
Bakchios (potter)	2	—	—
Kittos (potter)	1	—	—
Kittos Gr.	4	—	—
Charikleides Gr.	3	—	—(plus 1 frag.)
Hobble Gr.	2	—	—
Nikomachos Series**	19	—	—
Similar	1	—	—
Bulas Gr.***	—	—	36 miniatures

*At least twenty-six red-figure painters employed Panathenaic shapes. However, since these works were in the red-figure technique and resemble Panathenaic prize amphorae in shape only, they are omitted from this list.

**This series contains most of the vases with the names of Archons inscribed after Athena was faced to the right, (i.e. after 360/47 B.C.)

***Included here for convenience.

APPENDIX V

TYPES OF LIPS, FEET AND HANDLES
(mentioned in the text)

TYPES OF LIPS:

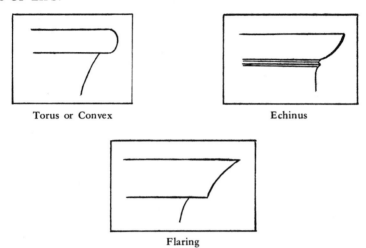

Torus or Convex

Echinus

Flaring

TYPES OF FEET:

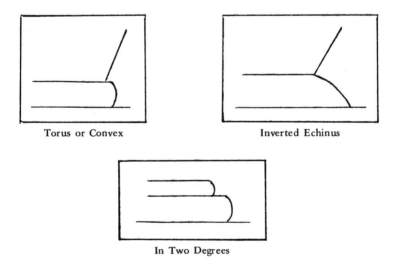

Torus or Convex

Inverted Echinus

In Two Degrees

TYPES OF HANDLES:

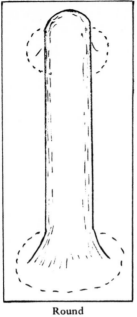

Round

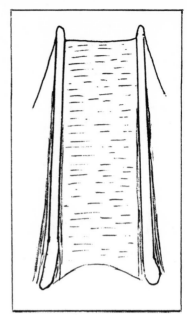

Flat-Flanged

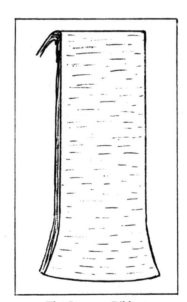

Flat-Strap or Ribbon

GLOSSARY OF TERMS

(Not already explained in the text)

AEGIS
: A breast-plate worn by Athena with a Gorgoneion and fringed with snakes.

ANIMAL STYLE
: A style of painting in which animals predominate.

APOTROPAIC
: A term used for objects that supposedly avert evil.

ARCHAIC PERIOD
: c.a. 700-480 B.C.

ARCHON
: A chief magistrate of ancient Athens.

ASKOS
: A small flask with circular body, wider than high, with a convex top and an arched handle reaching from one side across the top to a spout on the other side; size: 5-15 cm. (2-6 inches); used for containing oil.

BILINGUAL
: Term denoting pots on which one field is in black-figure and another in red-figure.

CHITON
: A lightweight sleeved tunic, usually of linen, worn by women.

CLASSICAL PERIOD
: ca. 480-323 B.C. (for vase painting, usually divided into Classical 480-420 B.C., Late Fifth Century, and Fourth Century).

DEFLOCCULA- TING AGENT
: See peptizing agent.

ECHINUS
: A convex molding — See Appendix IV.

ENGOBE	: See slip.
GEOMETRIC PERIOD	: ca. 900-700 B.C.
HELLADIC, LATE	: See Mycenaean.
HELLENISTIC PERIOD	: ca. 323-27 B.C.
HIMATION	: A heavy mantle or cloak usually of wool.
HUMAN STYLE	: A style of painting in which human figures predominate.
KALPIS	: A one-piece hydria (so-called to distinguish the shape from that of the normal neck-hydria).
KOMOS	: Revel.
KOTHON	: See plemochoe.
KOTYLE	: See skyphos.
KYATHOS	: A ladle in the form of a deep cup with one tall vertical handle.
LEKANIS	: A flat bowl with a cover, two handles set horizontally, and a rim to receive the lid.
LOUTROPHOROS	: Usually a form of amphora with two handles, but sometimes a form of hydria with three handles; tall and slim with a long neck and flaring mouth; used at weddings and at funerals for unmarried persons.
MASTOS	: A deep cup shaped like a woman's breast.
MERRYTHOUGHT	: A British name for wishbone.
MYCENAEAN PERIOD	: Late Bronze Age in Greek lands; the same as Late Helladic ca. 1550-1100 B.C.
OBVERSE	: The opposite of reverse; the side of a vase with the main painting.
OLPE	: A slender oinochoe with a sagging belly.
PELIKE	: A one-piece amphora with a sagging belly and broad mouth.

160

PEPLOS	: A heavy sleeveless garment, usually of wool, worn by women.
PEPTIZING AGENT	: A substance such as potash, which when added to a fine solution of clay, breaks down coagulation of particles making the solution thinner and more fluid (see protective colloid below).
PHIALE	: A low, stemless, shallow cup without handles used for drinking and pouring libations; often it had a central boss.
PLEMOCHOE	: A vase with a turned-in rim, a high foot and lid; it was used for carrying perfume for use in bathing and in religious ceremonies.
POLOS	: A cylindrical or pill-box hat.
PROTECTIVE COLLOID	: Agents such as humin (found in urine, gall, and sour wine), which by tanning action prevent recoagulation of the particles after they have been released by a peptizing agent.
PROTO-ATTIC PERIOD	: ca. 710-610 B.C.
PROTOGEO-METRIC PERIOD	: ca. 1050-900 B.C.
PROTOME	: The upper part of a human figure or the forepart of an animal.
PSYKTER	: Similar in shape to an amphora, but without handles, or a double-walled type of amphora with a spout; used for cooling wines.
RESERVED	: Left in the color of the clay.
REVERSE	: See obverse.
SEMI-OUTLINE	: Partly black silhouette and partly outline.
SKYPHOS	: A deep cup with two horizontal handles with no stem and a low or pedestal base (also known as a kotyle).

161

SLIP	: Liquid clay applied as a coating on a vase prior to firing.
STAMNOS	: Similar to a one-piece amphora, (but with the neck reduced to a mere collar), high shoulders and horizontal handles.
TONDO	: A disk or circular picture inside a kylix.
TORUS	: A convex molding — see Appendix IV.

BIBLIOGRAPHY

Arias, P.E., and Hirmer, M., *A History of Greek Vase Painting*, Thames and Hudson, London, 1962. A very large volume, profusely illustrated with textual coverage of the major painters.

Beazley, J. D. and Ashmole, Bernard, *Greek Sculpture and Painting to the End of the Hellenistic Period*, Cambridge, University Press, 1932.

Beazley, John Davidson, *Attic Black-figure: A Sketch*, Proceedings of the British Academy, Vol. XIV, Humphrey Milford Amen House, E. C., London, University of Oxford Press, Oxford, 1930. A lecture delivered in 1928.

_____, *Attic Black-Figure Vase Painters*, Oxford, Clarendon Press, 1956. The authoritative work on Attic black-figure painters, the works attributed to them, groups of items, classes of items, potters' names, love names, etc. . .

_____, *Attic Red-figure Vase Painters*, Oxford, Clarendon Press, 1963, Vols. I-III. The authoritative work on Attic red-figure painters, the works attributed to them, groups of items, classes of items, potters' names, love names, etc. . .

_____, *Paralipomena: Additions to Attic Black-figure Vase Painters and to Attic Red-figure Vase Painters*, Oxford, Clarendon Press, 1971 (2nd Ed.). As indicated in the title, this last work by Sir John Davidson Beazley brings his two former classic works up-to-date.

_____, *Potter and Painter in Ancient Athens*, Proceedings of the British Academy, Vol. XXX, London, Geoffrey Cumberlege Amen House, E. C. 4, 1946. A lecture delivered to the Joint Meeting of Classical Societies at Oxford in 1942, revised and expanded. An interesting brief (43 pages) discussion of the works of potters and painters and how they worked.

_____, *The Development of Attic Black-figure*, Sather Classical Lectures, Vol. 24, 1951, University of California Press, Berkeley and Los Angeles, 1951, Cambridge University Press, London, 1951. An excellent summary of the subject.

Boardman, John, *Greek Art*, Frederick A. Praeger, Publishers, New York, Washington, 1964 (Reprinted 1965). One of the Praeger World of Art Paperbacks; devoted to Greek art in all forms. See especially pages 89-102.

Bothmer, Dietrich von, "Andokides the Potter and the Andokides Painter," *Bulletin*, The Metropolitan Museum of Art, New York, February, 1966.

163

————, "The Painters of Tyrrhenian Vases," *American Journal of Archaeology*, Vol. XLVIII, No. 2, 1944, The Archaeological Institute of America, Rumford Press, Concord, N. H.

Carpenter, Rhys, *Greek Art: A Study of the Formal Evolution of Style,* University of Pennsylvania Press, Philadelphia, 1962. See especially pages 85-91 on symmetry of Greek vases.

Caskey, L. D., *Geometry of Greek Vases,* Museum of Fine Arts, Boston, 1922, (Communications to the Trustees V). An attempt to provide evidence from Attic black-figured and red-figured pottery in the Boston Museum of Fine Arts in support of Jay Hambidge's theory that Greek artistic design was based on geometric principles.

Cook, R. M., *Greek Painted Pottery,* Methuen and Co. Ltd., London, 1960. A readable and comprehensive survey of Greek painted pottery from the Protogeometric period to the Hellenistic period with special sections on shapes, techniques, inscriptions, chronology, potting, the history of the study of vase painting, etc.

————, *The Greeks Till Alexander,* Thames and Hudson, London, 1961. A general survey of history, politics, economics, society, arts, etc., of the ancient Greeks.

Devambez, Pierre, *Greek Painting,* The Viking Press, New York, 1962. One of the Compass History of Art series. Well illustrated with a brief text dealing primarily with Greek vase painting, but covering painting from Cretan to Roman times.

Droop, J. P., "The Dates of the Vases Called 'Cyrenaic' ," *The Journal of Hellenic Studies,* VOL. XXX (1910), published by the Council of the Society for the Promotion of Hellenic Studies, MacMillan and Co., London, 1910. See especially pages 21-27 dealing with what are now called "Droop Cups." Professor Droop considered these to have been made under Laconian influence.

Folsom, Robert S., *Handbook of Greek Pottery: A Guide for Amateurs,* Faber and Faber Ltd., London, 1967. A guide to Greek pottery from the Protogeometric period to the Hellenistic period covering styles and shapes.

Hambidge, Jay, *Dynamic Symmetry – The Greek Vase,* Yale University Press, New Haven, 1948 Ed. Excellent for cross-sections of Greek vases showing symmetry of forms.

Haspels, C. H. E., *Attic Black-figured Lekythoi,* (membre étranger de l'Ecole française d'Athènes) E. de Boccard, Paris, 1936, 2 Vols. A definitive study of black-figured lekythoi (Beazley's ABV makes important additions of items attributed to the various painters).

Herford, Mary A. B., *A Handbook of Greek Vase Painting,* Univ. of Manchester Press, Longmans Green & Co., London 1919. An historical account of Greek vases from the Cretan period to the late Italiote, with chapters on potters and painters, shapes and uses — now out-dated.

164

Hoppin, Joseph Clark, *A Handbook of Greek Black-figured Vases,* Librairie Ancienne Edouard Champion, Editeur, Paris, 1924. A listing of Proto-Corinthian, Corinthian, Boeotian and Attic black-figured masters arranged alphabetically by painters within groups, listing items attributed to them with descriptions, sketches and photographs. An added chapter deals with South Italian red-figure masters.

Kitto, H. D. F., *The Greeks,* Penguin Books, Inc., Baltimore, 1965.

Lane, Arthur, *Greek Pottery,* Faber and Faber Ltd., London, 1963. A brief, but well-illustrated and concise summary of Greek pottery from the Protogeometric period to the Hellenistic period.

Noble, Joseph Veach, *The Techniques of Painted Attic Pottery,* The Metropolitan Museum of Art and Watson-Guptill Publications, New York, 1965. An excellent work dealing with the making and decorating of ancient Greek pottery. Very well illustrated and very readable, it is a "must" for anyone interested in Greek pottery.

Payne, Humfrey, *Necrocorinthia,* Clarendon Press, Oxford, 1931. A massive tome dealing with Corinthian art in the Archaic period.

Pfuhl, Ernst, *Malerei und Zeichnung der Griechen,* P. Bruckman A.G., Munich, 1923. A massive work.

_____, *Masterpieces of Greek Drawing and Painting,* translated by J. D. Beazley, MacMillan Company, New York, 1926. Contains selections from the above to present a collection of masterpieces in photographs.

Richter, Gisela M. A., *A Handbook of Greek Art,* the Phaidon Press, London, 1960, (Especially pp. 279-289 and 305-325). An excellent summary of Attic black-figured pottery in a work covering all phases of Greek art.

_____, *Attic Red-figured Vases: A Survey,* The Metropolitan Museum of Art, New York and Yale University Press, New Haven, 1958 (Rev. Ed.). An authoritative work on Attic red-figure artists, and the development of the red-figure technique.

_____, and Milne, Marjorie J., *Shapes and Names of Athenian Vases,* The Metropolitan Museum of Art, New York 1935. The definitive work on shapes and names of Attic vases.

Robertson, Martin, *Greek Painting,* Skira, Geneva, 1959. A well illustrated survey of Greek painting with special emphasis on painted pottery.

Schoder, Ramond V., *Masterpieces of Greek Art,* Studio Books, London, (undated). Devoted to all ancient Greek art forms. This book contains some excellent illustrations of black-figured vases.

Ure, P. N., "Droop Cups," *Journal of Hellenic Studies,* Vol. LII, Part I, 1932, Council of the Society for the Promotion of Hellenic Studies, London, June, 1932. A special study.

Vermeule, Emily and Chapman, Suzanne, "A Protoattic Human Sacrifice?" *American Journal of Archaeology,* Vol. 75, No. 3, July, 1971, The Archaeological Institute of America.

165

Walters, H. B., *History of Ancient Pottery,* Charles Scribner's Sons, New York, 1905, (3 volumes). A monumental work covering Greek pottery in general, sites, discovery, uses of clay, shapes, history, subjects portrayed, etc., plus Italian vases.

Webster, T. B. L., *Potter and Patron in Classical Athens,* Methuen and Co. Ltd., London, 1972. As indicated by the title this is a study of the influence of buyers on pottery production.

INDEX

171